REVIVING

REVIVING

GREAT HOUSES FROM THE PAST

Stephen Crafti

Photography by Gorta Yuuki

images
Publishing

Published in Australia in 2012 by
The Images Publishing Group Pty Ltd
ABN 89 059 734 431
6 Bastow Place, Mulgrave, Victoria 3170, Australia
Tel: +61 3 9561 5544 Fax: +61 3 9561 4860
books@imagespublishing.com
www.imagespublishing.com

National Library of Australia Cataloguing-in-Publication entry:

Author: Crafti, Stephen, 1959–
Title: Reviving : great houses from the past / Stephen Crafti.
ISBN: 9781864704655 (hbk.)
Subjects: Architecture, Domestic – Australia.
               Dwellings – Australia – Remodelling.
               Buildings – Australia – Repair and reconstruction.
Dewey Number: 728

Production by The Graphic Image Studio Pty Ltd, Mulgrave, Australia
www.tgis.com.au

Pre-publishing services by United Graphic Pte Ltd, Singapore

Printed on 140gsm GoldEast Matt Art by Everbest Printing Co. Ltd.,
in Hong Kong/China

IMAGES has included on its website a page for special notices in relation
to this and its other publications. Please visit www.imagespublishing.com.

CONTENTS

INTRODUCTION

The result of renovating a period home is often to obliterate any signs of the past. Many Victorian homes renovated in the 1950s and '60s, for example, had their entire façades remodelled. Off came the wrought iron lacework and 'fussy' decorative window surrounds. New square aluminium windows not only 'cleaned up' the design, but provided more light. And all that iron lacework across the verandah was simply catching dust anyway, wasn't it?

These radical solutions to renovating period homes were thankfully redressed in the 1980s, as the gentrification of many inner-city areas began to take place in cities worldwide. Victorian terraces had their lacework replaced and verandahs were restored with floor tiles approximating the original.

This book doesn't include homes from the Victorian period, but looks at homes from the more recent past, starting at 1900 and ending with 1950. The popularity of homes from these decades, which are being cleverly reworked to offer contemporary spaces, has been growing.

The houses featured in this book are all extremely different, in both style and scale. Some are large, almost palatial. Other homes are little more than what were once referred to as 'worker's cottages'. However, irrespective of size or location, these houses exemplify a number of different approaches in their renovation.

Most of the homes in this book appear original from the street. There may be a sign, such as a vibrant green side fence, indicating that something contemporary lies beyond. However, in line with council requirements, the heritage paint schemes have been carefully researched along with fences and other features of the façade.

This book features homes from each decade of the first half of the 20th century. Some homes were recently renovated; others were renovated a few years ago. Those renovated earlier, such as Kerstin Thompson's warehouse or Alexander Tzannes' design for a 1940s house, clearly illustrate that great design isn't bound by the passing of time, but by talent. Undoubtedly Chenchow Little Architects' recent reworking of a small cottage will be appreciated well into the future. Not necessarily the latest or

most expensive renovations – these homes have been beautifully reworked to suit contemporary living and the way the owners prefer to live.

Understanding each design is fundamental to this book. Like contemporary fine art, it's important to get into the mind of the architect. Why were certain decisions made? What challenges were faced in combining the past with the present? Just as important is being able to understand and articulate the client's brief. For any renovation to succeed, it must reflect the lifestyle of the owners.

The book opens with a modest cottage in Mosman, Sydney. Built circa 1900, it appears relatively intact from the street. There have been few alterations to the original design at the front of the house, apart from a space for off-street car parking. However, when the front door is opened, there's an impressive vista through to the back garden. And although there are some decorative features from the past, a new steel structure, painted off-white, is just as intricately detailed.

Kerstin Thompson's Drum, in a warehouse in inner Melbourne built a few years after the Mosman cottage, is considerably larger in scale. Originally a sheet metal factory, this building has been transformed into a home, but still incorporates elements from the past, including pressed metal ceilings and large timber trusses. The interior design also reflects the owners' interests, and incorporates many exquisite fabrics, objects and artefacts found on their travels to India. Bringing the past and present together does, however, present challenges. In the case of this warehouse, Thompson removed some of the original timber trusses to create an internal courtyard.

A warehouse-style space, previously a school hall, has been magically transformed by Multiplicity. Built in 1912, the building appears to have weathered beautifully. The slate roof is still intact, as is the front door. In the entrance is a timber bench. Although clearly new, it is easy to imagine that a similar bench may have existed there once, covered with children's school bags. And while the school desks and tables are long gone, elements from the past remain. The kitchen island bench, for example, was previously used in one

of the classrooms. In the bedroom, new joinery was designed to suggest old-fashioned school desks with lift-up lids.

Andrew Maynard's renovation of a building of similar vintage also respects the past while building on the future. Maynard's design for a house in North Fitzroy, Melbourne, creates a sharp division between past and present. Beyond the ornate plaster arch in the central passage is a new steel-and-glass breezeway. To heighten the transition between the two periods, there's a dramatic change in ceiling height. Maynard also sharpened this division with the choice of materials, as well as the use of colour. Vibrant lime green and red joinery features in the new kitchen and living areas. And unlike the home's original pitched roof, the new wing is curvaceous and wrapped in timber.

Each home in this book is significantly different, but there are distinctive hallmarks common to a certain period. Tanner Architects and interior designer Louise Bell, for example, renovated a substantial house in Bellevue Hill, Sydney. Designed in 1923, it has a strong Arts and Crafts feel that was common at the turn of the 20th century.

With massive fireplaces and chimney pots, it has a solid and earnest feel. But the house has been completely reworked by the architects and interior designer to create a lighter, considerably less foreboding interior.

Designer Piero Gesualdi preferred a moodier fit-out for his own home in Melbourne. Once a drill hall, the building is now both a home and an office. Dark timber flooring and dark walls envelop the visitor upon arrival via a black steel-clad entrance. Original built-in timber joinery and Art Deco mouldings add richness to the building.

Some of the homes featured in this book were not originally architecturally significant, allowing the owners and architects to be less restricted. However, other homes such as the Leslie Wilkinson house in Double Bay, Sydney – which was carefully restored and renovated by architect Luigi Rosselli and interior designer Louise Bell – came with a high pedigree. How does a designer pay homage to a great architect while still maintaining a vision that allows for contemporary living? This fusion is successfully

achieved on both fronts, with the pièce de résistance being a clean and minimal contemporary pavilion perched at the top of the Double Bay site.

Houses from the 1940s are also featured in this book. Designed by Douglas Snelling, one Sydney house of this period 'moves forward' in an extremely sensitive manner. Architect Alexander Tzannes made the most subtle changes in the original part of the home. As well as containing the home's original hallmarks, many of Snelling's furniture designs, both built-in and freestanding, have been incorporated. And on the lowest level, overlooking the harbour, is an impressive guest wing.

As time moves on, homes from the first half of the 20th century are becoming increasingly more valued and there is now a greater appreciation of how to both restore and renovate these homes. However, it is not only the designs, both past and present, that resonate, but also the stories about how these homes came to be as they are today, and the often arduous process of both peeling back and adding layers to reveal and create such architectural gems.

1900–19

With the advent of a new century, house designs became simpler. The often heavy features found in the Victorian period were replaced with lighter, less-fussy ornamentation. Along with this simplification came an increasing appreciation for natural light. Heavy drapes were replaced by fine lace curtains. Rather than the focus on the fireplace in living rooms, there was a gradual acceptance that the garden offered a pleasurable aspect.

Given the age of homes built between 1900 and 1909, it is not surprising that many require considerable reworking, from kitchens and bathrooms to living areas. Fortunately, many of these homes still retain their exquisite leadlight windows, wide skirting boards and cornice detailing.

A CHANGE OF PLAN

Circa 1900   **Remodel: Nest Architects**

Situated behind a chunky timber mullion fence is a temple-like villa. Faded with time, its earthy façade, with a decorative parapet and distinctive niches, is a drawcard for locals. Located in the inner-city suburb of Fitzroy, Melbourne, the house was occupied by squatters for several years. Sadly, 90 percent of the house burnt down before the current owners took possession. 'We were planning to renovate the place, just adding a few modern amenities', says the owner, who lives in the house with his partner and their two young daughters.

WILLIAM CANDY

The house has a fascinating history. Originally built in 1863, the cottage was significantly extended in the early 1900s. Only the stable remains from the original build. William Candy, a local stonemason, who constructed many cemetery headstones, built what was then known as 'Boston Villa' as his family home. 'Descendants continually ring our

bell. Some have even given us old photos of the place', says the owner. 'The story is that the family once ran a linen business from here, delivering goods by horse and cart', he adds.

After the fire the only thing remaining was the façade, including the original stables, and a few brick side walls. Nest Architects had presented the couple with a scheme for minor renovations before the fire. But afterwards, an almost entirely new house was conceived. Architect Emilio Fuscaldo, director of Nest Architects and his colleague Imogen Pullar discovered a variety of bricks on the site, some handmade. They also discovered chiselled blocks, now lining some of the front garden beds.

PLANNING RESTRICTIONS

Designing a contemporary house behind a period façade didn't deter either the architects or owners. However, planning restrictions requiring setbacks did limit the opportunity

to expand the house beyond its current footprint. The architects thought about extending a first floor to sit immediately behind the original parapet, but the local council required greater setback from the street. Other variations to the architects' design included a number of cladding options. Zinc in a charcoal grey was originally mooted, then a rusted Corten steel. 'Our clients settled on timber. Timber has a certain warmth. It's also not overly precious', says Fuscaldo, who was mindful of creating a relaxed atmosphere in the house that would accommodate two young children. The timber used to clad the new house, a combination of mahogany and stringy bark, will eventually grey and blend in more with the original façade.

A LOOSE BRIEF

Although the owners have an innate understanding of design, they didn't hand the architects a formal brief or send them a catalogue of images found in magazines. They simply spoke of the number of rooms required and being mindful of how the

family live. 'When we saw the design, it ticked all the boxes, including space for a wine cellar', says the owner, opening a door in the kitchen leading to a set of stairs. 'We also didn't want the new wing to overshadow the villa,' he adds.

While the architects were keen to design a contemporary home, they were respectful of the past. The room built around 1900, for example, was fully retained. The external façade was maintained, with only new French-style doors punctuating the southern elevation. As the front garden functions as the main play area for the children, the architects were mindful of providing direct access to the garden, as well as increasing natural light. However, the two sets of doors are framed by new concrete reveals, connecting back to the original façade. They also open to a beautifully landscaped garden, created by Matt Nees.

The original entrance to the home was via a front door, through what was once the stable. However, given the family's preference for a more casual style of living, the main entrance was placed to the side of the house, past the original front rooms. This not only creates a sense of arrival, but also allows the form of the 20th-century structure to be fully appreciated by the owners and visitors. More importantly, the location of the front door allows the family to enter the middle of the house rather than walking through a long formal passage.

The new entrance/front passage also separates the original front room, used as a living room, from the new wing. The fire ripped through this room, eliminating most of the original features (with the exception of two arched niches). While the living room

appears original, it was 'put back together' with appropriate materials and features of the period. Cornices were sympathetically matched, as was the ceiling rosette. The marble mantle surrounding the fireplace was also replaced. But rather than selecting one without any blemishes, the architects chose a hearth that is slightly worn. New tallow wood floors were also instated, in a narrow width suggesting age, and simply oiled.

FASCINATING COLLECTION OF FURNITURE, ART AND OBJECTS

As the owner regularly travels to Europe to source 20th-century furniture and objects for his stores, it's not surprising to discover a wonderful array of unusual pieces in his house. 'It's almost a showcase for the owner's showrooms', says Fuscaldo, pointing out the 1950s armchairs, a 1970s Perspex floor lamp, as well as a rusted steel stool that came off a tractor. And reflecting the couple's preference for the relaxed rather than the stuffy, the chandelier in the living room is decorated with the children's cardboard puppets.

MAIN BEDROOM

Also in the original part of the house is the couple's main bedroom. Once the stable, it was given a new front door, window and verandah at the turn of the century. But as with the living room, the fire left behind the walls only. With the renovation came new timber floors, laid on a heated slab, as well as new windows, double-glazed for thermal efficiency. The architects also designed an ensuite bathroom and walk-in dressing area for this bedroom. And although some of the detailing, such as the narrow recycled tallow flooring (from the seating of Waverley Park football stadium), was expensive, other features, such as the joinery in the walk-in wardrobes, came from IKEA. To create a more crafted effect, the architects clad the dressing area in messmate timber.

The ensuite bathroom is also a fusion of new and old. The terrazzo basin, circa 1930s, had been in the owner's back rooms at work, waiting to find a use. And although new, the white wall tiles are evocative of many of the bathrooms designed in the early part of the 20th century. According to Fuscaldo, it wasn't just about choosing the appropriate materials, it was important to create the right ambience in every space. 'Each space should have its own identity, as well as a unique quality of light', says Fuscaldo. The bedrooms, for example, are darker and calmer, while the living spaces are considerably lighter and linked to the outdoors. The bathrooms, including the ensuite to the main bedroom, are illuminated only by a skylight, creating an almost meditative environment.

Emanating from the west, the light in the living areas creates a different ambience. Spread across the rear of the site, the new wing includes a dining area, a central kitchen and a play area/television room for the children. Above the kitchen is a guest

suite, used by family members when they come to visit. This bedroom, ensuite and mezzanine-style living area will be used by the children when they move into their later school years and require a separate study.

APPROPRIATE SCALE

While the living spaces are generous, they tie in with the scale of the original rooms of the house. Rather than design the living areas as one large open space, with a kitchen at one end and living areas at the other, the architects created a number of fluid spaces that feed into each other. The children's television area, for example, can be completely screened by a large timber sliding door when the owners prefer not to hear the television. Likewise, the dining area is contained, with sliding glass doors allowing access to the courtyard. 'I'm not a fan of open-plan spaces. It can be particularly awkward if you want your own space', says Fuscaldo.

The arrangement of spaces also allows the couple's collections to be thoughtfully displayed. The dining room, for example, features display units from the early part of the 20th century. There's an impressive display of glass and ceramics, as well as more ubiquitous items, such as a straw basket. Indigenous totem poles are unexpected features, as are as Marion Drew's provocative photographs of road kill.

AT THE CORE OF THE HOUSE

The kitchen, located at the centre of the house, is robust. A stainless steel benchtop, found in a salvage yard, complements a white tiled splashback. And to add texture, as well as warmth, the messmate-clad wall conceals a fridge and pantry. As with other rooms in the house, there's a wonderful fusion between new and old. Pendant lights above the kitchen's central island bench are from the early 1960s.

As the house occupies the rear portion of the site, the architects were mindful not to create a 'back-of-house' feel, with the garage and children's bedrooms simply worked

into the residual space. Both structures are clad in mahogany and stringy bark, their pavilion-like forms creating an idyllic backdrop to the internal courtyard. To create a subtle division between the children's bedrooms and television area is a metre-wide light well/garden, planted with agaves. 'It was crucial to get light into the living areas rather than face a blank wall,' says Fuscaldo, who also increased the amount of light with a generous skylight above the kitchen.

AVOIDING THE GLASS BOX

The courtyard was treated as an outdoor room and a dining area, as much as a place to simply relax. With 1950s planters and crazy paving throughout, there's a sense of post-war Palm Springs rather than temperate Melbourne. One of the architects' concerns was that the extension didn't read as simply a glass box tacked onto the back of a period home. Considerable time was spent in articulating the rear façade, with its multitude of sliding timber doors leading to the courtyard. To allow the new spaces to

'breathe', a double-height space was created between the kitchen and the rear sliding door. This not only animates the living spaces, but allows for greater transparency throughout the house, including the mezzanine guest suite.

KEEPING THE FAITH

The fire certainly caused a major rethink by both owners and architects. Though while this caused a major setback and change of direction, it proved a favourable result. 'I think part of the success was the trust our clients placed in us. They are entrenched in the design world, but there was always that faith', says Fuscaldo. 'Let's face it, why hire an architect in the first place if you're just after a drafting service', he adds. The results are certainly testimony to this.

A SHEET METAL FACTORY

Circa 1900   **Remodel: Kerstin Thompson Architects**

Once a sheet metal factory, this spacious warehouse in inner-city Melbourne is now a unique home. Bought several years ago by the owners – Ron and his partner Beth – this conversion was in the vanguard of warehouse living at the time. 'Now developers tend to subdivide these types of spaces and try to fit as many units as possible', says Ron.

From the street, the red-brick building appears relatively discrete. Painted signage from its previous life still remains, as does the cobbled bluestone paving in what was once the delivery area. However, as the garage door to the warehouse slides across, the scale of this property starts to unfold. An inflatable plastic mannequin of Edvard Munch's *The Scream* is an appropriate warning that one's adrenaline is about to shoot upwards.

Reworked into a home by Kerstin Thompson Architects, the award-winning design beautifully combines the past with the present.

LEAVING A PERIOD HOME

Beth and Ron previously lived in a large National Trust home nearby, where they raised three daughters. It was large enough, but Beth felt the interior was 'heavy'. 'Many of the ceilings were gold leaf and the focus in most of the rooms was towards a fireplace. It was poorly lit with insufficient natural light', says Beth.

OPENING THE DOORS

The family may well have remained in their large period home, had Beth not driven past this warehouse just at the time the garage doors were open. She could see the depth of the space even from her car. The warehouse covers most of the site (50 by 125 metres). When Beth returned home, she rang a friend who was a real estate agent to make an approach. Fortunately for Ron and Beth, the sheet metal business that had started on the site in the 1950s was in decline, with many of its workers moving further from the city as a result of the gentrification of the neighbourhood.

After the owner had consented to sell, Ron and Beth then had to secure an architect. Rather than choose one immediately, the couple invited two architects, including Kerstin Thompson, to present them with a scheme. While they hadn't seen Thompson's work before, Ron and Beth could instantly see it was the stronger of the two, although not exactly what they were after. 'Kerstin also seemed to have a greater understanding of the area, as well as the building. I think it was also her intellect. She has a commanding way of communicating her ideas', says Ron, who admits it's difficult for him to conceptualise spaces in plan form (although Thompson did present them with a model of her design). The other trait that appealed was Thompson's ability to understand the couple, and how they live. 'It wasn't just about creating an architectural statement', says Beth.

AN ABUNDANCE OF SPACE

To begin with, 'there was almost too much space. The footprint was enormous, too vast for a comfortable home', says Thompson, who was keen to balance the building's industrial grandeur with domestic intimacy. Thompson's many challenges included increasing the amount of natural light, as well as defining what appeared to be an endless space.

GRADIENT SPACES

One of the few images shown to Ron and Beth was a museum in Nouméa, New Caledonia, designed by Renzo Piano. This drum-like building, clad in timber battens, provided a starting point. While Ron couldn't quite understand the connection, Beth was able to visualise the idea of a drum being inserted into the warehouse. Thompson also spoke of 'gradient spaces', with areas being loosely defined rather than put into boxes. 'You're not aware of leaving one space and moving into another. There are few, if any

boundaries', says Ron, who also appreciated the luxury of removing space. The drum-shaped courtyard area formed within the warehouse is approximately 700 square metres in area.

The drum, which is slightly off-centre, allows the spaces to be fluid and intimate. The space in the dining area is deliberately generous to allow for entertaining on a grand scale. 'The shutters and windows within the drum can be shifted to allow for guests to wander through the entire space', says Thompson.

PRESSED METAL CEILINGS

Entry to the home is via a modest lobby, with original pressed metal ceilings and walls. Even the original windows separating the lobby from the garage remain. The front timber door to the warehouse is also still intact – the door pockmarked from the factory workers using it as a dartboard during lunch breaks. Charcoal-black steel was inserted into this lobby space, framing a staircase as well as enclosing a new powder room for guests.

The dark and moody lobby, originally used as an office for the sheet metal business, opens to a spacious dining and living area. Featuring exposed brick walls, with flecks of paint from its previous life as a factory, the warehouse features large timber trusses cut back to allow for the insertion of the new central courtyard. Beth and Ron trusted Thompson's judgement to cut back the tresses from the courtyard area, but there was some initial trepidation. 'We can see now she was right. Removing the trusses from the courtyard provides greater transparency through the entire space', says Ron, who enjoys seeing the open fire in the living area from the other side of the courtyard, particularly when it rains.

DEFINING THE SPACES

As well as 'cutting out' the middle of the warehouse to create a courtyard, the architect created subtle divisions in the space using partition-like steel-clad walls. At the front of the warehouse, for example, is Ron's study, and beyond the courtyard, towards the rear

of the warehouse, is Beth's. These areas are casually discovered moving through the space, rather than appearing as fixed, highly defined areas.

Likewise, the kitchen, extending the width of the courtyard, doesn't follow the pattern of a traditional kitchen. While there's an island bench with a stainless steel bench top, the majority of preparation is relegated to a galley-style area adjacent to the kitchen. Concealed by a steel-clad wall, this area includes sinks, ovens and generous cupboards for storage. Like the end of the kitchen bench, painted in a deep purple hue, the cupboards in the 'scullery' are finished in a striation of rich hues, from purple to orange and saffron, evocative of the colours of India. Ron and Beth regularly travel to India, and presented Thompson with a number of coloured powders they'd purchased while there. 'I've had a long association with India. I've been travelling there since I was 20', says Ron, showing the packets of powder he bought from an Indian market. These colours explode not only literally at the Indian festival of Holi, but also figuratively in the jewel-coloured saris worn by Indian women.

'Beth spoke about the kitchen being "loose". The circular courtyard really enabled this fluidity. It's not like a square or rectangular courtyard that creates more rigid spaces', says Thompson.

A TOUCH OF INDIA

Other features in the warehouse also reveal the couple's love of India. Coloured glass pendant lights over the dining table were purchased on one of their trips. Indian artefacts appear on many of the walls. And instead of curtains, many of the windows are covered with dhotis, ceremonial saris edged with gold thread that are trditionally worn by Indian men.

The 'drum' courtyard, truly pivotal to the design, is one of the ways Thompson conceived the spaces. This courtyard, framed with steel-and-glass windows and doors, features operable timber screen shutters. The shutters not only diffuse the light, but also animate the interior as they are moved either vertically or horizontally across the glass walls.

SHOWCASING CONTEMPORARY ART

Notable in the warehouse is the presence of contemporary and Indigenous Australian art. Robert Owen's sculpture and paintings are well represented on the walls. Owen's work can also be found on the concrete floor within the courtyard. Titled *Galaxy*, the sculpture shows the family members' birthdays represented in the cosmos, with inlaid concrete paths joining the 'stars'. Other artists whose work is featured in the warehouse include Janet Laurence, Rosemary Laing, Paddy Bedford and Freddie Timms. A life-size image of a kangaroo by Reko Rennie adds humour to the space.

MIXING FURNITURE STYLES

The furniture in the house is as diverse as the artworks. The formal dining area (although hardly formal) features a Biedermeier table and chairs, and the lounge is complemented by a contemporary lounge suite from B&B Italia. On the other side of the courtyard,

and regularly used when friends and family come over, is an English-style dining suite. The kitchen features a country-style dresser. 'Kerstin helped us to rationalise some of the furniture from our previous home. She didn't try to talk us out of bringing many of the pieces with us. She thought these spaces needed to include things we considered precious to us', says Beth.

According to Thompson, her clients were initially hesitant to follow the path of contemporary architecture. 'They thought it would be cold and impersonal. I reassured them that we could create something contemporary that responded to the way they live. Why should they get rid of all their furniture just because they move house?' she asks.

While the original brick walls, literally hosed down with high-pressure water, reveal the building's original grain, new windows and skylights allow for increased light. Thompson

also improved access to the rear garden via elongated French-style doors. In the main bedroom located on the first floor to the rear of the house are jewel-coloured slot windows, added to allow northern light while animating the interior.

MAIN BEDROOM SUITE

The main bedroom suite, accessed via a circular steel staircase, includes the main bedroom and sitting area, as well as a dressing area and large ensuite bathroom. This bathroom features distressed brick walls as well as an angled mirror over a vanity to capture the sky and a roof deck. Beth and Ron suggested to Thompson that the ensuite bathroom should evoke the sense of a wash house, reminiscent of India. To capture this flavour, the windows are framed by dhotis and the floors are marble, a material often used in India.

UNDERSTANDING THE CONTEXT

While there are touches of India in this home, Thompson, as Beth appreciated from the start, understands context. A slot window at the rear of the home frames a slender gum tree that's become a landmark in the area. On the side of the bedroom is an angular portal-style window that frames the local town hall. 'Kerstin really set up so many vistas of the neighbourhood', says Beth, who with Ron, enjoys overseeing the area from the various decks, as well as the 'lookout' tower accessed from the guest wing at the front of the warehouse. And unlike their previous house, where the view was internalised, here the focus is towards the garden or the surrounds, with light, as well as shade, adding richness to the interior spaces.

GLIMPSES OF MIDDLE HARBOUR

Circa 1900   Remodel: Chenchow Little Architects

THE SEARCH

The owners of this house in Mosman, Sydney, took two years to find their abode. Unsure about what they wanted, they inspected everything they could in countless locations. 'We kept changing our mind. We were buying in a rising market and places we thought we could afford became out of reach', says Esther, who lives in this house with her husband Simon and their four-year-old son.

POTENTIAL TO RENOVATE

The owners wanted not only an inner-city home, but also a house with potential to renovate, together with off-street car parking. Esther stumbled on this semi-detached house while commuting to work across town. Fortunately the home's peeling white painted façade didn't deter her. Or the fact that it is located on a fairly busy thoroughfare. What it offered were three bedrooms, off-street parking and a garden, although the latter featured an outside toilet and laundry. The house was also orientated to the north

and had a gentle 2.5-metre slope from the street. A frangipani growing through the rails of the upstairs balcony sealed the deal.

NO MCMANSION

The brief given to Chenchow Little Architects was to open up the house completely. The couple wanted to rid themselves of the pokey rooms, many of which were dark. Mildew appeared on one of the interior walls. 'We didn't want a McMansion style house, just a place that was light and open, where we could entertain', says Simon. They also mentioned to architects Tony Chenchow and Stephanie Little that they had a strong preference for an all-white minimal interior, recalling the great German philosopher Goethe's words 'colour is the pain of light'.

Simon and Esther's wish list also included generous storage (to enable them to live in a minimal house) and a built-in coffee machine. Simon also wanted his own room – a study or office where he could read and listen to music.

When Chenchow and Little presented their scheme to their clients, the concept was there, although Esther found it difficult to interpret the drawings. As a consequence, the architects returned with a three-dimensional model of the proposed renovation. The 'floating' all-white form featured exposed trusses and a dramatic cantilevered balcony. One of the few features in the original scheme that was altered by Simon and Esther was the tilt-up glass garage door. This was considered an unnecessary cost that would have exceeded their budget.

As the house is located in a heritage street, the original façade was retained. The turned timber columns were painted, as well as the brickwork. And in keeping with the period, the front garden was landscaped in a traditional English style, with clipped hedges. However, once past the front door it is clear that any 'cobwebs' from the past have been removed.

Chenchow Little Architects retained the two original front rooms of the Mosman house, one of which is used for Simon's study/music room, the other as their son's bedroom. Complete with decorative moulded ceilings and open fireplaces, these rooms are almost completely intact. The architects also retained the decorative archway in the passage.

NO SHOTGUN CORRIDORS

According to Chenchow, one of the greatest challenges in renovating terrace homes is avoiding the 'shotgun' effect, the long narrow passage appearing to extend indefinitely. As this house is only 5 metres wide, creating a sense of width was fundamental to the redesign. As soon as the front door is opened, the eye is drawn past the corridor towards a tree in the back garden.

Apart from the home's façade and two front rooms, very little remains of the original. As the house slopes 2.5 metres towards the rear fence line, Chenchow Little was able

to create a third-level extension. From the street, there is no sign of this third level as it is concealed behind the pitched steel roof. 'Council regulations meant any new work couldn't be detected from the street', says Chenchow.

CONNECTING TO THE GARDEN

One of the problems with the original house was its disconnection from the garden. Originally, at ground level there were little more than outbuildings. Chenchow Little excavated further into the site to create a second living area. Complete with large sliding doors and a generous covered deck (provided by the cantilevered balcony), this room enjoys both northern light and a leafy outlook. Furnished simply with a module lounge and an Eames lounge chair and ottoman, it appears considerably lighter and larger thanks to the mirrored walls. Ceramic floor tiles also ensure the space is low-maintenance, ideal for the couple's young son.

A FLOATING PLATFORM

On the central level of the Mosman house are the kitchen and living areas. Like the living area below, the kitchen features a mirrored wall. This also brings light into the core of the house, as well as creating an illusion of something beyond. To accentuate depth, a 9-metre-long bench extends to the end of the living area. Featuring a white Corian bench top and white MDF painted cupboards this multipurpose unit appears to float in the space. At one end of this bench is the kitchen sink, while the other end has ample storage for books and toys. To ensure a minimalist aesthetic, the fridge, freezer and pantry are concealed behind kitchen doors. Chenchow Little was also able to provide a cocktail bar in the dining area, with a flip-down door appearing flush with the dining room wall.

The most distinctive features of the renovation are the exposed steel trusses along both walls. This technique, which harks back to the post-war period, was used to ensure a 3-metre cantilevered terrace/balcony was possible. Chenchow and Little acknowledged the importance of working closely with a talented structural engineer, in this instance Damian Hadley from Simpson Design Associates. 'Architecture and engineering are intrinsically interwoven. We couldn't have achieved this design without him', says Chenchow. The expressed beams, also painted white, not only made the design possible, but set up an industrial aesthetic.

MINI-ORB CEILING

To complement the beams, Chenchow Little used mini-orb (rippled steel) for the ceiling. Unlike many renovations, where joints are concealed, the ceiling in this house features exposed screws and the doors also feature piano hinges. One of the problems in using unorthodox materials was raised when the builder started fixing the mini-orb. Initially lacking sufficient screws, the ceiling tended to droop. 'I was quite alarmed when I first saw the roof. At one point, I thought I should have gone with plaster', says Esther.

In keeping with the minimalist approach, the furniture is relatively sparse, but carefully considered. Two plywood and leather armchairs designed by Hans Wegner complement a white leather lounge. In the dining area, there is an Alvar Aalto dining table with Eames plywood chairs. A pendant light by Louis Poulsen completes the arrangement.

While a completely white interior may throw some off balance, it's a perfect vehicle to explore the changing light. The extensive shading system, comprising motorised aluminium shutters on the deck, allows for a continuous play of light. These shutters also allow for privacy from neighbours. 'We were conscious of overlooking, but it was important to ensure the deck could be used year-round', says Chenchow. Light also creates intricate patterns on the elongated frosted-glass window above the kitchen bench. Accentuating the trees, this glass takes on the appearance of lace at certain times of the day.

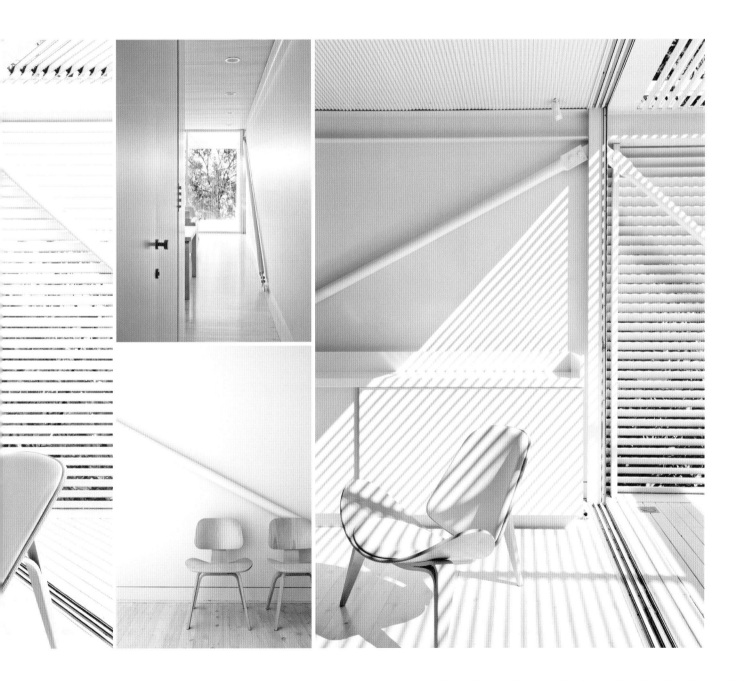

THIRD LEVEL

As the house slopes away from the street, the architects were able to include a third level. This level features the main bedroom, ensuite bathroom and a generous dressing area. Though it was not anticipated, the owners as well as the architects were delighted to discover glimpses of Middle Harbour from the floor-to-ceiling bedroom window. The architects conceived the top level, with its three-sided frameless glass balustrades, as 'walking through a floor plate', like a hole cut through a floor. They were keen to maximise sun protection with external aluminium blinds.

DETAIL

This house appears relatively simple at first glance – a white extruded box joining a period home. However, on closer inspection, the devil is in the detail as much as the

broad brushstrokes. Chenchow Little Architects didn't just create a line where the past meets the present. The ceiling in the passage is finished with plaster on one side of the decorative archway, and on the other side it features mini-orb.

'The new and old are interlocked rather than being in separate camps', says Chenchow. Also considered was the treatment of the floors. While timber appears throughout the central level, the existing cypress pine in the original part of the house is in its natural colour. In the new section, the floors are limed, complementing the white interior, and where the two periods intersect in the passage, the direction of the floorboards changes.

Some friends and family were taken aback when the renovation was first unveiled. Some found it difficult to believe that people could live comfortably in such a minimalist home. 'It's extremely easy to live in. There are few surfaces to wipe and we've taught

our son to put his toys away after using them', says Esther. And while their 4-year-old son quickly learnt that the mirrored wall was an illusion, Esther's 90-year-old grandfather initially thought there was another room beyond the kitchen.

Probably the main challenge comes at Christmas time, when colourful decorations come into the stores. 'Thankfully, you can still find a white Christmas tree and white decorations', smiles Esther.

19

Many homes from this period, and the decade before, featured floral motifs that originated in the Art Nouveau style. Web-like plaster motifs, along with bevelled and leadlight glass, continued to create a romantic feel in homes. Red brick was often used in construction, with stucco detailing around windows and doors adding relief to the façade. Spaces were more fluid and the shotgun corridor through the centre of the house was becoming a less dominant feature.

A CLASSIC EDWARDIAN

Circa 1910   Remodel: Andrew Maynard Architects

A SIGNPOST

Originally built in 1910, this Edwardian house in North Fitzroy, Melbourne, is one of many in this quiet leafy street. From the outside, the only sign that something new has been added is a lime green and timber batten wall on one side of the house. 'It's just a small signpost', says architect Andrew Maynard, who was commissioned to transform this home for a couple with two young children.

ORIGINAL FAÇADE

Apart from the lime green 'wink', the Edwardian façade remains intact. The cast-iron lacework and leadlight glass over the front door are original, as are the tessellated tiles on the front verandah. The red-brick façade is punctuated with roughcast concrete. 'It has great bones. It just wasn't designed for contemporary living. And there was little connection to the garden', says Maynard.

The owners, Fraser and Rosemary, who have two young children, were previously living nearby. While their large Victorian home had sufficient bedrooms (four in total), there was no off-street car parking and only a small courtyard garden. The entire site was approximately 140 square metres, whereas this new property is just over 500 square metres, substantial for an inner-city location.

IN THE SAME FAMILY FOR 50 YEARS

Many looking for a family home close to the city often look further out of town. But Fraser was cycling past this house and noticed a forthcoming auction sign. Owned by the same family for 50 years, the house had been unsympathetically extended in the 1970s. Loosely designed in the Spanish Mission style, there was an arch linking the past to the '70s. The kitchen was a composite of orange floral tiles and timber joinery. Heavy drapes reduced any light filtering into the home to a trickle.

'That didn't faze us. Rosemary and I loved the original house. It was well located for the local school and near our extended family', says Fraser.

Rather than rush into a renovation, the family lived in the house for a couple of years. They were conscious of its shortfalls, such as the lack of natural light (the back garden is orientated to the south rather than the north). But they knew this could be addressed by the right architect.

SELECTING AN ARCHITECT

Andrew Maynard was not only the right architect for the job, he was also the closest architect to the couple's previous home (occupying a studio a couple of doors away). 'We'd seen a few of Andrew's renovations and appreciated his adventurous approach. He also seems to think outside the square', says Fraser.

THE BRIEF

While Fraser and Rosemary didn't have a clear image in their minds of what the house should look like, they were conscious of being able to entertain their extended family (occasionally having 18 people for dinner). They also wanted the house to be fairly robust for their two young daughters. Rosemary also had a short wish list that included a walk-in wardrobe, an ensuite and a large bathroom for the girls. Fraser also had to have a garage for two cars and his bike. Unlike many clients, who present their architect with a series of magazines with earmarked pages, there were no style guides.

A FEW IMAGES TO START WITH

Maynard showed the couple images of a Japanese home in Tokyo, which had a roof garden. Another home had a more Scandinavian feel and was extensively clad in timber. 'They seemed to warm to elements in both homes', says Maynard, who used these images as a starting point for renovating the North Fitzroy house.

One thing both the architect and owners were keen to ensure was that the outdoor spaces were not sacrificed to increase the home's footprint. Maynard was also mindful of the shadowing effect that would result from adding a second storey to the house, given its orientation on the site.

LIGHTLY TOUCHING THE ORIGINAL ROOMS

The original front rooms of the house were retained. With high ceilings and wide skirting boards, these two rooms are now used by the children. One of the rooms is a shared bedroom, while the other is a play area, complete with new built-in shelves. The central passage separating these two rooms has simply been restored, including the decorative arch plasterwork. However, the following two rooms, forming part of the original Edwardian house, have been modified.

ACCOMMODATING A SIDE PATH

The room previously used as the formal lounge is now the main bedroom. In keeping with Rosemary's request, there's an adjoining walk-in dressing area on one side of the room, and an ensuite bathroom on the other. These two areas are clearly new, defined by lime green painted 'pods'. While these two spaces marginally increased the home's footprint, the side garden/pathway was rarely, if ever, used. It had become a repository for everything from rakes to the girl's toys. To retain a sense of a garden outlook, a small courtyard garden was created between the two pods.

On the other side of the passage, directly opposite the main bedroom, is an additional bedroom, ideal for guests. Alternatively, this room can be used as a library or quiet space for the family to retreat to. Although the original proportions of this room remain, Maynard inserted a new glass door to a side garden to increase light and strengthen the connection to the outdoors.

Creating a contemporary wing to a period home is always a challenge for architects. Does one blur the transition between past and present? Or should there be a strong juxtaposition in style between the two periods? In this instance, the architect created a clear distinction between the two. A breezeway made of rusted steel and glass separates the two volumes. Featuring stackable glass doors, this breezeway opens to an internal courtyard. With its Astroturf lawn and lemon tree, this area acts as a 'breathing space'. The doors are pulled back during the warmer weather to allow the blurring of the indoor/outdoor spaces. The architect also deliberately lowered the ceiling height of the breezeway (to 2.3 metres) to strengthen the division between the past and contemporary designs.

The new wing, clad in spotted gum, is a refreshing deviation from the glass box solution that is often attached to period homes. While a rectilinear solution may have been

the cheapest solution, it would not have made such an impact. The curved structure was conceived by Maynard for a number of reasons, one of which he says is a result of three females living in the house. 'A glass box would have given the place a more masculine feel. These curved edges are more feminine. But they also make the addition seem more like a garden pavilion', says Maynard.

PSYCHO THRILLER

Separating the new kitchen, dining and living areas are the main bathroom, laundry and study area. The bathroom, with its frosted glass door, borrows light from the courtyard, as well as from highlight windows in the study area. Maynard was also keen to introduce some whimsical elements into the design. Both bathrooms, for example, feature white and red tiled walls and floors. In each are also built-in vanities, made of plywood with red laminate bench tops. 'I was inspired by Alfred

Hitchcock's film *Psycho* says Maynard, who refers to the arrangement of bathroom tiles as like splattered blood.

The red used for the study area is more contained, surfacing as bright red laminate embedded in the white built-in laminate desk. Fraser's study in his previous home was a room with a door. This study allows him to work (both he and Rosemary are in the catering business) while being able to keep an eye on their two children.

ELEMENTS FROM THE PAST

Maynard was also keen to retain a sense of the past in this renovation. An original red-brick wall frames one side of the courtyard, complete with remnants of paint that appeared on what was once a living room wall. The arched doorway linking the study to the kitchen also formed part of the previous owner's renovation in the '70s. 'I think it's

important to recall memories of past design. It's part of the home's history', says Maynard.

VIBRANT COLOUR

The new kitchen, with its 7-metre-long central island bench, also acts as an important bridge between the original and new designs. Clad in stainless steel and lime green laminate, this joinery also provides a colourful addition to the house. The curved edges to this central unit are echoed in the stainless steel splashbacks. As the owners are in the catering business, they are well aware that stainless steel appears at its best after a few months of wear. 'The steel appears like glass when it first arrives. The first scratch is evident. But after there are a few, it gains a certain patina', says Fraser. The choice of materials for the kitchen and living areas also provide a contrast between materials used in the rest of the renovation – spotted gum, rusted steel and polished concrete

floors. 'The laminates have quite a synthetic feel, in contrast to many of the natural materials', says Maynard.

A TELEVISION IN THE GARDEN?

To further ground the playfulness of the lime additions, Maynard included a stained black timber bulkhead in the kitchen area, together with cladding some of the joinery in spotted gum. Other details, such as the porthole windows in the rear façade, further animate the living areas. The built-in joinery in the lounge, reminiscent of an inverted skateboard, also brings a smile to visitors' faces. Fraser enjoys recalling the story of a young neighbour entering the space for the first time. 'Apparently he asked his parents why the people next door have a television set in their garden!' says Fraser, pointing out the grass-green shag pile carpet and the garden effect when the doors on either side of the lounge are completely pulled back.

Originally Maynard presented plan to create a two-storey pavilion at the rear of the site. There was going to be a second storey above the garage, which would have functioned as a studio/roof terrace. However, this proposal would have exceeded the couple's budget. So it was decided to simply clad the rear double garage with timber battens, allowing access to a roof terrace.

ROBUST FURNITURE

Given there are two young children who love exploring the place, the house is simply furnished. However, the furniture has been thoughtfully considered with vibrant coloured dining chairs. The armchairs in the lounge may not be designer classics, but Maynard appreciated the way they were selected for their curved timber armrests, complementing the many curved timber features in the home.

CHALLENGING THE BUILDER

Although completed within budget, this renovation wasn't simple. While Fraser and Rosemary embraced Maynard's design, the builder did occasionally show signs of stress in dealing with the many curves presented to him. 'I could see him suffering at times', says Maynard, who was also aware that concepts such as 'splattered blood' amused the owners far more than the guy who laid the tiles in the bathrooms.

A TOUCH OF THE '70S

While the extension is clearly contemporary, there's a sense of the 1970s, both in the colour scheme, as well as in the many delicious curves throughout the house. However, rather than revisiting the '70s that one prefers to forget, the slight references celebrate the best of that period. And from the street, this classic Edwardian home fits into its heritage streetscape perfectly, offering only a glimpse of what lies behind this front door.

Circa 1910

WESTWYCK – SUSTAINABLE STYLE

circa 1912   Remodel: Multiplicity

This school in West Brunswick, Melbourne, is slowly being transformed into a community of like-minded people. With an emphasis on sustainable design, the development, known as WestWyck, includes vegetable gardens and bicycle storage facilities. Owners Mike Hill and his partner Lorna Pitt transformed what was once the school's hall (built circa 1912) into their home. 'The school was designed in the late 1880s. This hall was originally the school's quadrangle, where presumably all the children would assemble', says interior designer Sioux Clark, a co-director of Multiplicity, who worked closely with her life and business partner, architect Tim O'Sullivan, on this project.

The complex is presently divided into seven apartments, the eighth space being the former school hall, and there are plans for Multiplicity to transform the remaining classrooms into further homes. 'We were keen to attract families as well as couples to the development. An apartment doesn't have to be small and segregated. We also want

the grounds to be used by everyone', says Pitt, who engaged landscape artist
Mel Ogden to create a sustainable, drought-resistant, contemporary garden.

FIRST IMPRESSIONS

From the street, the school hall (formerly used for art and recreation) appears almost
intact. However, the Art Nouveau-style façade, with its decorative fretwork and mossy
tiled roof, has undergone minor changes. When Multiplicity first inspected the building,
three sets of front doors had been boarded up. These hoardings were removed and
replaced with timber doors found discarded on site. Sanded to reveal the original paint,
these central doors set the tone for the renovation. 'In our work, we are keen to reveal
the history of a place, even if surfaces are slightly worn and imperfect. Tim and I also
enjoy providing a sense of what came before. You can almost imagine all the children
dropping their bags at the entrance and reaching for their art smocks', says Clark.

While children's bags and coats aren't found in the entrance to what is now a home for Hill and Pitt, there is a timber-slatted bench that extends into the living areas. And although the walls have been painted, the architects strove to retain as much as possible of the original building. Glazed Art Nouveau tiles remain on the walls in the entrance, as well as in the adjacent office, which doubles as a bedroom. Some of the wall tiles are slightly stained, but they create a rich patina, as do the cast-iron hydronic heaters salvaged from some of the classrooms.

Translucent Perspex screens are a hallmark of Multiplicity's designs. A screen separating the office area allows diffused light from the entrance. WestWyck, the name of the school, as well as that adopted by the developers, was founded on a platform of sharing sustainable ideas with the community at large as well as within the 'school grounds'. Plywood joinery in the office, for example, is used in its original state rather being treated

with a finish. And the screws holding together the Perspex-and-steel screen allow elements to be dismantled and reused. 'Mike and Lorna wanted the spaces to be as flexible as possible. This room (currently the office) could also be used for guest accommodation or as another living area', says O'Sullivan.

FLEXIBLE SPACES

The idea of flexibility is carried throughout what is essentially the one large space that makes up this home, comprising the open-plan kitchen, dining and living areas. Only the powder room, wrapped in plywood and Perspex, is enclosed at ground level. Multiplicity's brief was to maximise natural light, as well as draw out the building's past, as much as it was to create a contemporary home.

While the soaring timber-lined ceiling immediately attracts attention, it is the details that resonate. Original decorative steel tie rods suspended from the ceiling (designed to

keep the roof structure taut) are as distinctive as the ornate coloured leadlight windows at either end of the building. One of the challenges for the architects was drawing in northern light through these windows, once fixed. The solution was to take them out and allow them to sit on pivotal steel window frames. An additional layer of sashless double-hung windows creates a balcony effect when the leadlight doors/windows are left ajar. A place to enjoy the northern light, the 'platform' inside these windows functions as the perfect reading room. A lectern-style plywood balustrade framing this space allows for magazines and newspapers to be spread out.

RECYCLED MATERIALS

One of the most noticeable features of this renovation is the use of recycled materials. Adjacent to the kitchen are raised stainless steel doors. O'Sullivan had found these former lift doors in a laneway. 'They're quite dense, ideal to insulate wine. But the doors also reflect light', says O'Sullivan, who regularly looks in dumpster bins and salvage

yards for materials. While some things can be used immediately for a renovation, other materials are stored and brought out when a suitable project arises.

The centrepiece of the kitchen is an island bench. Originally used by students for their artwork, the table remained unused in the hall for decades. Multiplicity raised the table on steel stirrups to ensure it was the correct bench height. They also extended it by adding a stainless steel sink and plywood drawers. To allow Pitt to display her collection of earthenware, the architects designed a stainless steel shelf that cleverly links the two elements together. Also expressed in the kitchen is the stainless steel range hood, which is supported on a steel frame. Steel racks allow kitchen appliances to be reached easily. 'We prefer using a limited palette of materials, such as plywood and acrylic. We wanted to express the structures and materials, from both the past and present', says Clark.

Plywood features in the open shelves and drawers, separating the kitchen from the staircase. Acrylic sliding doors allow some items, such as food, to be concealed, while other parts of the unit reveal its contents. One of the most poetic features of this design is the smoke-coloured acrylic used at the rear of the joinery. Teapots and ceramics displayed on the shelves are presented in a play of shadow and light.

Like many of the materials used in this renovation, the furniture is lightly distressed. Simple steel and timber dining chairs were salvaged from some of the classrooms. And the velvet armchairs have been in the family for years. The steel shelving unit, now used for crockery, was reworked from an original school locker. Where new furniture was required, pieces were designed by the architects. Plywood bench seats in the living area, for example, can also be locked into position to create an additional bed, should guests come to stay. The unit also thoughtfully connects to the plywood window reveals, providing an ideal location for curling up with a book.

A SENSE OF THE 1950S

Multiplicity will often have just the right material stored in their warehouse from previous renovations. One of the few elements in this renovation that wasn't recycled is a wrought-iron screen enclosing the staircase. The wrought iron has a distinctly 1950s feel, evocative of the lacework attached to homes in the neighbourhood.

The screen design also has an uncanny resemblance to the original tie rods (circa 1912). 'Similar design features are often reinterpreted at different times in history. But its how you interpret these that creates a contemporary edge', says Clark. In contrast to the 1950s-style wrought iron, the screens enclosing the 'boardwalks' on the first floor are made from steel poles. These poles not only allow for unimpeded views through the space, but also complement the original vertical lining boards.

READING PLATFORM

As well as accomodating a reading platform, the first floor is also home to a mezzanine study, wrapped in plywood and acrylic. There is also the main bedroom, complete with pod-like ensuite bathroom. These mezzanine additions were among the few structural changes that had been made to the hall prior to this renovation, and although the architects and clients agreed on their retention, they had to be reworked. The balcony reading area was originally a curved shape, detracting from the rectilinear form of the building and its original features.

MAIN BEDROOM

Like the reading platform on the northern edge of the building, the main bedroom, located to the south, is also delineated by lectern-like shelves. Made from plywood

and acrylic, this joinery was inspired by old-fashioned desks with lift-up tops. The acrylic surfaces provide a window or display area for hats and gloves, as well as for more precious objects. 'When we design a piece of joinery, we're keen for it to have two functions; in this case, it's storage as well as forming a balustrade', says O'Sullivan.

Steel shelves found in one of the classrooms are now used for storing clothes, and while there is sufficient hanging space in the bedroom, there is also an old retail rack for clothing. These elements add a rustic layer to the bedroom, as do the multitude of ceramics and artefacts that are arranged on the bedside tables also designed by Multiplicity. There is a small terrace leading from the bedroom, providing an opening that also allows for cross-ventilation, particularly during the warmer months of the year.

The bathroom pod in the main bedroom also provides a number of functions. Plywood joinery on either side of the pod features cupboards and drawers, and provides a screen

for the bathroom. Keen to ensure light could penetrate into this area, the architects included a sliver of acrylic between the plywood joinery. A pivotal translucent door to the bathroom also allows for filtered light. The architects were keen to ensure that original details, such as the decorative tie rods, could be appreciated from all vantage points in the home, including the mezzanine study.

A HIDDEN SPACE

While most of the spaces within the home can be seen instantly, there is an unexpected attic, accessed via a steel ladder adjacent to the study. Originally unused roof space, this area was lined simply with plywood walls. The original chunky timber trusses are impressive, as is the length of the space. Used as a study nook or as an extra bedroom for guests, this whimsical space is certainly worth the climb.

SUSTAINABLE PRINCIPLES

Most of Multiplicity's projects are renovations. In almost all cases they inherit another period or style of building. As with this school conversion, they are always respectful of embodied energy and the need to invest in materials that have had a previous life. For the owners, this renovation was more than simply an exercise in reusing materials. Entirely committed to sustainable principles, the couple was keen to create a community in what was once a school. Tradespeople, for example, were selected not simply on the basis of their skills, but also their proximity to the site, thereby minimising energy costs associated with transport. The developers were as keen to reduce the carbon footprint with every decision made, from energy-saving appliances to recycling water on the property. 'Everything we've done is probably contrary to real estate advice you would normally get', says Pitt.

1920–19

29

Most houses built in the first half of the 20th century did not follow a specific 'house style'. In the 1920s, for example, design styles ranged from Tudor Revival to Spanish Mission and Californian Bungalow. Many homes built during this period still possessed many of the Arts and Crafts features that appeared in the early part of the 20th century. Timber strapping and built-in joinery became more important as decorative plaster frieze work declined in popularity. Many of the homes built during this period had a distinctively English feel, with built-in fireplaces and wall sconces.

THE SCALE

Circa 1923   Original architect: John Peddle, Peddle Thorp
Remodel: Tanner Architects

FIRST IMPRESSIONS

Gary and his wife Mahshid (known as Max) made the decision to purchase this large home in a day. They were living in Tokyo with their four children and were looking to return to Australia in the near future. After living in an apartment in Tokyo with four children, the scale of this house in Bellevue Hill, Sydney, on a 2,200-square-metre site, would have been overwhelming. 'I could clearly see the house needed a huge amount of work, but the size of the house, as well as the land, was impressive', says Gary.

RETURNING FROM TOKYO

When the family moved into the house on their return from Tokyo a couple of years later, the home's imperfections became more apparent. It wasn't just the dated interior, last renovated in the 1970s and '80s, that was the problem – the additions were also poorly considered. A glass-roof conservatory added to the western side of the house couldn't be used after 4 pm when the afternoon sun took hold. The swimming pool

was leaking and the tennis court was designated 'home court advantage', as the base consisted of artificial turf over a cork base and only those in the know could predict where the ball would ricochet.

TWO HALVES

From the outset, the Bellevue Hill house was a case of 'two halves'. The front portion of the house was relatively intact, albeit in poor condition, while the additions to the rear of the home were ill considered, both in terms of layout and orientation. Originally designed in 1923 by John Peddle, a director of Peddle Thorp (now PTW Architects), the house was a fusion of many influences, such as the Arts and Crafts style as well as the Federation style in Australia, popular in the early 20th century.

WHAT THE MARKET WANTS

Gary and Max weren't sure which architect to select for the task ahead. They'd interviewed a few, some recommended by friends. One architect even suggested that the house, constructed in dark brown bricks, should be rendered, like many of the homes in the neighbourhood. There were also comments made to the owners as to 'what the market wanted', as though rendering and painting bricks added cachet as well as value. Fortunately, Tanner Architects appreciated the value in the home's original bricks, as well as its design. 'The bricks (dubbed "liver bricks" as a result of their colour) create a unique character. They give the house a presence', says architect John Rose, a director of the practice.

THE BRIEF

While Gary and Max can't recall the exact words used to brief Tanner Architects, they were looking for an increased amount of light, a strengthening in the connection

between the indoor and outdoor areas, a solution that would 'tame' the western sunlight and, importantly, retain the home's character. 'Gary and I also wanted a contemporary design that responded to a family with four children', says Max.

Tanner Architects worked closely with interior designer Louise Bell, director of Interni, in reworking the house. 'The renovation had just started when we were called in. There was sufficient time for us to look closely at all the original detail, as well as how the spaces would eventually flow', says Bell.

As the western side of the house couldn't be 'rescued', it was removed completely. As well as being compartmentalised and not responding to contemporary living, ceiling heights were uneven and one of the few connections to the garden was via a hot glass pavilion that lacked any air conditioning.

THE 12-METRE CHIMNEY

Originally the Bellevue Hill house had a shingle roof, but similar shingles couldn't be found, so slate tiles were used instead. One of the other features fundamental to Tanner's design was the 12-metre-high brick chimney that could be seen from the street and was a prominent feature in the neighbourhood. In response to this feature, Tanner Architects designed an almost identical brick chimney on the western side of the house, also extending 12 metres in height.

EXTENDING THE OUTDOORS

One of the most significant changes to the original scheme was the addition of a generous outdoor awning to the west and north, extending 3.5 metres and 4.5 metres respectively. Detailed in copper, this awning could have made the kitchen and living areas appear relatively dark by today's standards. However, Tanner created a

continuous band of glass between the edge of the roof and the awning to allow light to penetrate the interiors. 'You're getting reflected light with this arrangement, rather than the full brunt of the western sun', says Rose. The architects, through engineering ingenuity, also ensured the verandah was free of vertical posts that impeded the view of the garden.

RESPONDING TO ART

'John (Rose) and I were working towards the same ideals for this house. We were both conscious of the home's strong horizontal lines. The leadlight windows have their own rhythm', says Bell. While the brief called for a robust contemporary home, the design also had to acknowledge an impressive collection of art, including: Howard Arkley, Fred Williams, John Olsen, Ian Fairweather, Rover Thomas, as well as sculpture by John Kelly, Robert Klippel and Vera Möller. 'We had to make sure there was sufficient

wall space for the paintings, as well as providing the correct lighting', says Bell, who recalls Gary not wanting a 'glass box' that would eliminate wall space to display their art collection.

CENTRAL STATION

While grand in terms of scale, it's a relatively informal house. Even the pivotal glass front door is rarely used, with the family preferring to enter the house from the rear. The back door leads to a space dubbed 'Central Station', which the boys use as a study. They drop their bags, remove their shoes and head straight to the kitchen, particularly during the school week.

The western wing now comprises one fluid, uninterrupted space, with a kitchen and dining area at one end, and an informal living area at the other. Over 20 metres in length, this informal living wing features limed timber floors and built-in joinery with

slatted door fronts along one side of the space. Casement windows as well as stackable glass doors to the verandah can be pulled back entirely to allow the indoor and outdoor areas to be used as one.

OPEN-PLAN LIVING

In keeping with Max's request for clean simple lines, the kitchen features a separate walk-in pantry/preparation area. And the central island bench, with its stone top, is treated as a piece of furniture, unencumbered by the usual sink. 'Max didn't want to have to see dishes next to a sink from the living areas', says Bell, who also concealed the fridge behind joinery, as well as an appliance cupboard. However, while the design is minimal, there is generous storage space by means of cupboards, as well as deep stainless steel drawers for pots and pans on either side of the commercial oven.

The built-in timber shelves framing the sliding doors to the formal dining room also create additional storage space, as well as a sense of depth between rooms. These shelves not only reinforce the solidity of the original house, but also create a buffer between formal and informal living spaces. To create privacy, as well as allowing light to penetrate, the sliding glass doors feature frosted glass.

NEW AND OLD FURNITURE

While the furniture in the home appears to have been carefully selected for each nook, it was a case of integrating the owners' existing furniture as well as acquiring new pieces such as the contemporary lounge suites. A few items, such as the English-style wingback armchairs in the study, were recovered. Some of the owners' pieces, such as the French dining table, have been placed in an alcove in the formal lounge. A Chinese tea box is now a side table in the same room.

Like the furniture, some of which has been given a new life, many of the original rooms at the front of the house have been reworked. The study adjacent to the front door, for example, was given additional windows in the same style as the original and grass wallpapers that create a light and textured effect.

THE LOBBY

The lobby of the home was also completely redesigned, including finishes and materials that provide a more fluid effect throughout. Timber floors replaced the black and white tiles that had been added in the 1970s. Tanner Architects also replaced the staircase with timber treads and an angular brass handrail with a bronze finish. 'The original timber balustrade was completely rotten. Part of it had even been burnt', says Rose.

Other changes to this area included a wine cellar where previously there was a powder room. And to one side of the lobby is a new guest powder room, together with a coat cupboard.

FLEXIBLE SPACES

Even though this house was designed for a couple with four children, the brief to Tanner Architects was to create flexible spaces. So while there are four bedrooms for the children, as well as a main bedroom, each room has an ensuite bathroom, making them suitable for guests, whether family or friends. One of the most impressive rooms on the first floor is the main bedroom, complete with its own walk-in dressing area and bathroom. While the scale of this bedroom is substantial, it's not overwhelming, partially as a result of the coffered ceiling and delightful box bay with its original leadlight windows. Although not obvious when arriving at the first floor, this area, including the main passage, was made significantly larger for two reasons: to increase natural light and to provide additional storage space. Another significant change was made to the attic, located on the home's third level. Previously used as a games room, this attic space was transformed

into a home theatre (normally relegated to a basement) and gymnasium, the latter offering a glimpse of Sydney Harbour. To ensure the children don't have to go up and down stairs between movies, the architects included a kitchenette.

GUEST WING

One of the few almost entirely new structures on the site is the detached guest wing adjacent to the tennis court. Apart from the shape of the pitched roof, almost everything else, including the manganese bricks, is new. To create a contemporary edge to the structure's traditional form, the architects included copper-clad dormer style windows on the first level. 'Originally there was a gardener's cottage, but it was fairly rudimentary. You had to lower your head every time you went upstairs', says Rose. This guest suite was specifically conceived for Max's parents who travel from the United States and spend

two to three months in Australia each year. As well as a sitting room with kitchenette, this area also includes two bedrooms and bathrooms. 'We based the design on the original structure, but it has been considerably expanded', adds Rose.

This is a grand house by most standards. However, in spite of the scale, it's understated. Although Max and Gary are delighted with the outcome of the renovation, you get a sense from speaking to Max that even in its original condition, she felt fortunate to be living here. 'I'd almost got used to the tape I put around the old dishwasher (preventing leakages). But when we started the process, we knew there would be something quite special at the end', she adds.

A CLEAR DISTINCTION

Circa 1928   **Remodel: F2 Architecture**

When the owners of this house first inspected it in 1998, it wasn't the architecture that left an impression. It was the home's solidity and construction that appealed. Built in 1928, the red brick home features solid walls and generous spaces. 'It just had the right bones. We knew that eventually we could turn it into something quite special', says Katrina, who lives in the house with her husband and their two adult daughters.

While there was no urgency to renovate the house, Katrina could see that if something wasn't done, the children would have left. It would then have been a large house for two people, and not quite right for them. Katrina still recalls sitting in the former living area, looking out through small panes. The pavement was red brick, like the house. Even the walls that framed the elevated swimming pool were red brick.

When architects Franco Fiorentini and Jeremy Schluter of F2 Architecture inspected the house, located in Toorak, Melbourne, they also appreciated its 'bones'. While it might have been an option to pull the house down and start from scratch, they both appreciated the detail and the craftsmanship in the original home. 'The house wasn't designed by a well-known architect, but it has some wonderful details. There's a mixture of the Arts and Crafts movement with the more geometric reliefs popular in the 1920s', says Fiorentini.

One of the problems with the house was related to the incline of the corner site. The front garden was approached via a set of stairs and even accessing the pool in the rear garden required climbing eight steps. This meant there were very few connections to the garden, and those connections were often through narrow doorways.

Although the house retained most of its original features, such as timber balustrades, skirting boards and cornices, the previous owner had done a number on the place in the 1980s. While the spa bath in one of the bathrooms wasn't a dire concern, the conservatory-style addition with its glass roof simply became a sweatbox in summer.

While the architects thankfully didn't need to start from scratch, they did remove the 1980s additions completely. With such a significant amount of red brick, the idea of extending using brick of any colour was never entertained by the architect or the client. Instead, zinc was selected to provide a clear distinction between old and new. The other reason the architects used zinc was that its colour could be found in speckled form in the home's original bricks. Also, like brick, zinc requires little maintenance. 'Both materials are quite noble. But together the two create a strong

contrast', says Fiorentini. This juxtaposition is also seen in the treatment of fences. The front fence, framing the original part of the house, is constructed of brick and steel rails. In contrast, the wall enclosing the garage and rear garden is rendered in charcoal, complementing the zinc-clad extension.

The original house featured terracotta roof tiles, but these had become brittle over time. The architects could have replaced them, but considered slate tiles to be a more elegant solution. Both types of tiles are found in homes from the same period. However, terracotta roof tiles are more commonly found in Spanish Mission-style homes (circa 1920), while slate lends itself to English-style homes, to which this house is closer in style. The slate also is more complementary to the zinc.

The front door retains its original frosted glass panel and the original tessellated tiles on the front porch are still intact. Beyond the threshold, the original entrance is also largely untouched. Complete with decorative cornices and pilasters framing entrances to rooms, there's a sense of craftsmanship. Angular vents with twig-like motifs in the formal living areas are as finely executed as the timber overmantle, with its hand-chiselled leaf design. Unfortunately, the timber in most of the windowsills had rotted. These were replaced in the original style, double-glazed for acoustic as well as thermal control.

Replacing the windows and doors also came with the need to rework the front garden, which was previously a considerable drop below. The architects took the opportunity

to create a front terrace through glass doors within the original bay window. However, apart from these changes, the formal living area at the front of the house remains essentially intact. The timber floorboards were simply rejuvenated. The adjacent study also remains as it was, including the antler motif on the fireplace surround, a stylised design that was popular in the 1920s.

A TRANSITION POINT

The stairwell, with its chunky timber balustrade and original pendant light, creates the transition point between old and new. But the chunky block-like wall separating the dining area from the new kitchen and living areas is an important feature in the unison between past and present. Finished in stucco lustro (polished plaster), one side of the joinery wall features open shelves for the display of objects. The other side, facing the dining room, is a cupboard for crockery. Although designed to appear as a free-standing object, this unit is framed by a toughened glass slot window and a sliding door

that disappears into a cavity wall. Solid in construction, this unit echoes the thickness of the walls, as well as the home's attention to detail.

CONTEMPORARY STYLE

The dining area is where the kitchen once stood – completely shut off from the meals and living area. One of the few changes made to this room was the creation of a box-shaped alcove with new doors to the terrace and garden designed by Jack Merlo. This makes the area more spacious, as well as removing the formality associated with dining in the 1920s. While the dining setting with its high-back chairs evokes to the past, the adjacent terrace with built-in barbecue and outdoor setting clearly responds to contemporary living.

As responsive to contemporary living is the new open-plan kitchen, meals and living area. Framed by floor-to-ceiling glass windows and sliding doors, there's an immediate

link to the garden with its lap pool and manicured lawn. An architectural dialogue is created with a second block-like wall, also finished in stucco lustro. On one side, this wall contains an alcove for a television set and built-in drawers, and on the opposite side is the laundry, together with storage areas. 'They're two "sister elements". It's not a big architectural idea, but these units express the craftsmanship of the original home', says Fiorentini modestly. 'They also reference the thickness of the original wall', he adds.

CLEAN MINIMAL LINES

The kitchen has been completely reworked. As well as a new island bench, made from stone and Calacatta marble, there are floor-to-ceiling two-pack painted cupboards. Like many contemporary kitchens, the fridge and pantry are within reach, but are located behind the second 'sister'. To complete the kitchen's clean and minimal lines, Nexus Designs included a simple white table combined with dining chairs by Patricia Urquiola.

Retracing the past, the alcove framing the leadlight window on the stairwell landing became another point of inspiration for the architects. Angular in form, its shape is picked up in some of the apertures formed within the zinc cladding. The form is memorable, as are the colours of the leadlight stairwell window, ranging from mauve to mint.

DRAWING IN THE CITY VISTA

Like the formal living areas and study, the main bedroom at the front of the house, with its adjacent retreat, has been sensitively reworked. Originally this bedroom featured heavy timber cupboards that eliminated the city vista. Now there are wall-to-wall cupboards, as well as an ensuite bathroom. Previously, access to this bathroom was from the hallway. The powder room, in a nook to one side of the staircase, is compact. Before, this pint-sized space was divided in two, with a separate area for washing hands.

SECOND LIVING AREA

Other changes to the upstairs rooms in the original part of the house included creating two separate bathrooms for the two daughters, as well as fitting both bedrooms with built-in desks. One of the main reasons for the renovation was to create a sense of independence for the daughters, allowing them to freely entertain friends and come and go as they please. As a result, the new section includes a second living area on the first floor, which leads to a covered terrace. While not a major design concern in the 1920s, cross-ventilation is fundamental to contemporary design. With the architects' scheme, there are windows with deep reveals in the daughters' living area. Likewise, there are large sliding doors leading from the living area on the ground floor to the bluestone terrace. When these doors are pulled back, there's a continuous flow between the indoors and outdoors.

For additional independence, there's a second staircase that leads directly to the kitchen and living areas. The stairwell features an impressive wall of seraphic glass, allowing natural light, but creating privacy from the street. 'The house can take our friends as well as our daughters' friends without either feeling in the way', says Katrina. 'We also wanted the design to stand apart from the original home. The two should work together', she adds.

A DIALOGUE

The combination of zinc and red bricks certainly creates an interesting dialogue between the two periods. The 1920s structure features a pitched roof, while the contemporary wing is rectilinear. Fiorentini doesn't compare his design to a piece of sculpture. 'This isn't that. The design was about making the spaces comfortable and engaging', he says.

As engaging as these spaces is the art within, with large paintings by Sally Gabori (in the informal dining area) and Euan Heng (in the formal dining, area above the fireplace).

As pointed out by Katrina, many people who renovate a home live in the contemporary part most of the time, and the original home is seen only by guests as they enter or leave. This certainly isn't the case with this family, who use their entire home, irrespective of formal or informal occasions.

Due to the effects of the Great Depression in the first half of the 1930s, many of the homes built during this decade are relatively austere. However, tough economic times often create a new ways of thinking, with inventive ideas replacing superfluous decoration. The Jazz Moderne style, evocative of streamlined cruise ships, became a strong influence on architects, largely a result of the efforts of legendary architects such as Le Corbusier and Walter Gropius.

CREATING A DIALOGUE

Circa 1932   Remodel: Denton Corker Marshall

Architect Greg Gong, a director of Denton Corker Marshall, says he bought the worst house in one of the neighbourhood's finest streets. Located in Malvern, a leafy Melbourne suburb, the street is lined with period homes, predominantly Edwardian. Complete with ornate fretwork and leadlight windows, these homes are much envied. However, the house Gong purchased, built in 1932 in the Depression era between the wars, was not one of these. On a relatively compact site (for the area) of 550 square metres, the modest home was orientated to the west, receiving harsh sunlight.

IN ORIGINAL CONDITION

Occupied by the same owner for almost 50 years, the house was presented to Gong in almost original condition. Apart from an ad hoc lean-to, little had changed over the years. As the Malvern house is in a heritage area, demolishing it wasn't an option. 'At least I

didn't have to go over someone else's renovation. I was starting from scratch', says Gong, who lives in this house with his wife Omega and their 10-year-old son, Felix.

While Gong didn't have to rework someone else's design, many of the features in the home had passed their use-by date. As well as replacing rotten timber floors, he also had to replace the window frames. Although the front windows appear original, they are actually replicas. New plumbing was also required, as well as stumping. Even the doors in the original part of the house were taken away and stripped of their layers of paint. One of the few original features that remains, the terracotta tiled roof, appears new. Gong left instructions to the roof cleaners to lightly clean the tiled roof, leaving the moss that had formed over many decades. However, 'they took the cleaning process too far, stripping the tiles of any growth', says Gong with disappointment.

FEW DECORATIVE FEATURES

Apart from the concrete stucco walls and tiled roof, only a few elements from the past remain. One of the few internal rooms left relatively intact is a front room, previously used as a bedroom. Now a study for Omega, this room includes its original proportions and doors, as well as brick fireplace. 'You can see it was a fairly austere house. There were no cornices or the decorative scrollwork that you often find in these homes', says Gong. 'It's virtually been gutted', he adds.

A SENSE OF THE PAST

Despite being almost gutted, there's still a sense of the past in the form of a corridor, a bedroom and the little amount of original detail that was preserved. Even the door accessories, such as handles, were replaced by Gong in a similar style to the original.

Elements of substandard or damaged quality were not retained. 'A lot of the original features were poor quality. It just didn't make sense to have to revisit these details later on', says Gong.

The formal living area, which formed part of the original home, was opened up. Previously this room comprised a lounge, a separate dining area and a galley-style kitchen. Access to the garden was via a single door. Replacing the brick wall with a single door is now a large picture window that overlooks the garden. Measuring 2.5 by 3 metres, this window forms an important junction between the original home and the new wing. Gong regularly uses the word 'dialogue' when describing the combination of old and new. From the new wing, the original house can be seen through this window; and from the formal living area, one can see into the present.

A RESTRICTED PALETTE

Rather than put up new divisions in the formal living area, Gong included a plinth made
from black Corian to create a centrepiece in the room. The plinth acts as a hearth for
the fireplace, as well as elevating the television set. This room, like other rooms in the
original part of the house, features limed oak floors and walls painted a natural white.
These walls appear cream, as distinct from a slightly sharper white used for the walls
in the new wing. While the half-strength difference isn't obvious, it does allow the past
to be seen as distinct from the present.

Void of cornices and decorative detail, the living room is furnished simply with a couple
of Chinese armchairs from the 1930s and a coffee table that was originally a Japanese
door. Two pendant Murano-glass lights from the 1970s, found in a vintage store,
add a contemporary feel to the interior. While this room is used for entertaining friends,

it functions primarily as a music room for Omega, a musician, who plays piano and violin. To maximise the view of the garden, Gong located one of the main structural supports to one side of the house, rather than allowing it to encroach on the picture window. This massive column is one of the few contemporary features visible from the street.

UNDER THE ORIGINAL ROOF

Within the footprint of the original home are two bedrooms, one with a new walk-in wardrobe and ensuite bathroom. Previously, the bathroom was accessed from the corridor. However, as well as being too small, it was also too basic. The new bathroom features generous glazing and light-wells, creating a sense of showering outdoors, and also allowing the original stucco and red-brick walls to be seen. There is a skylight extending the length of the ensuite to increase the amount of natural light.

A walk-in wardrobe increases the pleasure of dressing, with built-in sycamore shelves and steel racks on either side of the space. Gong could have designed built-in wardrobes

but felt the steel racks increased the sense of space, as well as allowing everything to be seen clearly in one glance. To ensure folded garments were easily identifiable, the timber shelves are backlit with translucent acrylic and fluorescent lighting.

Gong delineated the old and new with the floor finishes. In the original part of the house, all the floors are limed American oak and in the new wing, charcoal-grey basalt tiles were used. Providing further punctuation in the dialogue, there is also a slight change in level between the old and new. Although there is only one step between the two areas, there's a sense of entering a contemporary space.

OPENING TO THE NEW

One of the most dramatic changes between the past and present is a dramatic void, almost 6 metres in height, that extends the length of the open-plan kitchen, dining and living areas. Framed by equally high glazed windows and sliding glass doors, there's a strong link to the garden and terrace beyond. Gong also cleverly opened this living room

to the south with glazing. While there's a high brick wall delineating boundaries, a vista to a neighbour's garden, complete with mature trees, is still provided. 'It's quite an Asian sensibility to borrow views', says Gong.

ORIENTATED TO THE NORTH

While Gong's neighbours have orientated their home to the west in keeping with the orientation of their sites, the open-plan kitchen and living area in this house is orientated to the north to maximise winter sunlight. The kitchen is located at one end of the space and the lounge at the other, with all areas enjoying a balanced level of light from north and south.

A FLOATING KITCHEN ISLAND BENCH

The 4.5-metre-long central island bench in the kitchen is the first thing you notice when you enter the room. Suspended at one end by a singular steel beam, the Corian

bench appears weightless, almost defying gravity. Gong says that he wouldn't design a bench like this one for clients. This bench doesn't have cupboards below and the dishwasher is concealed behind joinery. This arrangement requires a little more effort by the family when rinsing dishes in the sink and putting them in the dishwasher. 'There are often a few drops of water on the floor that need to be wiped. We don't mind that extra effort, given the effect', says Gong. The island bench, complete with stainless steel sinks, also includes two sets of hot plates, one of which is often used for a wok. When the kitchen is not being used for cooking, the only thing on display on the kitchen bench is a goldfish bowl, containing one black fish.

Although there is no joinery below the island bench, Gong provided generous storage in the kitchen. One entire wall, made from two-pack MDF, conceals a fridge and dishwasher. This wall also includes storage for crockery and glassware, and as with all the joinery, there are no handles, creating a streamlined effect. The only division between the

cupboards are bands of sycamore shelving. This timber detailing in the wall of MDF cupboards also creates a strong visual connection to the wall of sycamore joinery fanning across the living area. To maximise storage space, Gong included a bank of built-in cupboards adjacent to the kitchen, which function as a pantry.

OLD AND NEW FURNITURE

Like most features in the house, there's a subtle combination of old and new in the furnishing. The dining table designed by Andrew Lowe, for example, is new, while the timber and leather chairs in the dining area are from the early 1960s, modelled on a Danish design. The lounge area is also loosely defined with an Eames chair and ottoman, together with a lounge suite and coffee table. This informal open-plan area was designed as a pavilion, clearly distinct from the original home. Elements such as the steel beam extending the length of the living area are visible. 'There is a trick in the way

the steel has been used. There are three steel beams across the span, with the central beam concealing the automatic blinds', says Gong.

NOT JUST A LAUNDRY

The renovation also provided an opportunity to create a functional and light-filled laundry. Located beyond the living areas, the laundry is framed by a floor-to-ceiling glass window on one side and a door to a small courtyard light well on the other. A bright red glass splashback animates the space and, as with the kitchen joinery, there are ample cupboards.

A RETREAT

On the first level of the new wing, accessed by American oak stairs, are a bedroom and bathroom for Felix as well as a generous mezzanine-style study/office for Gong.

The large office was always on the drawing board, and Gong enjoys both working and relaxing in this space, which is lined predominantly with books on architecture and design. The arrangement of the books is spontaneous, with only Gong able to put his finger on the right book instantly. An elongated table also allows Gong to spread out plans, as well as construct models for his designs. 'It's an extremely liberating space. I always feel connected to the family (when they're downstairs), as well as to the garden', says Gong. While almost all details were fixed well before construction commenced, Gong relocated one of the windows in his office to ensure unimpeded views to a neighbouring park.

Wherever one stands in this home, there's a reminder of the past. In Felix's bathroom, for example, there's a crisp outline of the neighbour's Edwardian home, complete with terracotta roof tiles, elaborate gargoyle and chimney pots. As well as floor-to-ceiling glass walls, there is a generous use of mirrored surfaces. Other vistas in the house are of the home's original rendered stucco and brick walls. 'It's not a particularly wide site (approximately 15 metres), so it's important to borrow the views and make the spaces feel as generous as possible', adds Gong.

FASHIONED WITH PRECISION

circa 1935

Remodel: Piero Gesualdi

FIRST IMPRESSIONS

Designer Piero Gesualdi is passionate about 1930s architecture, particularly the Art Deco period, but when he first encountered the building he now calls home, he found a fairly bland interior and exterior. Originally designed in 1935 as an army drill hall with associated offices, the building's location – in the inner-Melbourne suburb of Fitzroy – was its greatest attribute. 'I've always lived in the area. I couldn't imagine living anywhere else', says Gesualdi.

ORIGINAL STATE

The building was subdivided into five shells. The front portion, now occupied by Gesualdi, constituted the entrance to the drill hall (now a separate townhouse), an administrative office and a mess hall for army recruits. There was also a caretaker's residence located on the first floor. Self-contained with a kitchen and bathroom, this area contained three bedrooms. Comprising almost 600 square metres, including a wraparound terrace,

it was a rambling, cavernous space. 'This wasn't one of those grand Art Deco buildings. At the time, I wasn't drawn to any of the features, many of which had been painted over', says Gesualdi. 'Art Deco can be grand and imposing, but it can also be dark and oppressive', he adds.

As the building was fairly dark, many of the Art Deco features literally remained in shadow. The extensive timber skirting boards and doors appeared lacklustre, as did the bevelled glass in many of the doors. And while there was a substantial stone fireplace in what was originally used as the mess hall, it had become tarnished over time with a number of scorch marks.

Gesualdi had been renting the place for a couple of years before purchasing it. He was more or less camping, using a portable barbecue to cook. While he appreciated the space and the proportions of the rooms, initially he wasn't thinking of buying it. However, when the property went onto the market, he became weary of the groups coming

through to inspect it. 'It was more a matter of halting the inspections rather than actually wanting to buy the place', says Gesualdi.

DELAYS

When he purchased the property in 2001, Gesualdi didn't realise how long it would take to renovate the building. In the beginning he was not permitted to alter the exterior of the building, which was deemed to be of heritage significance by the local council, including the dimensions of the windows and even the modest steel front gate. 'You couldn't see the sky and there was no access to the garden. I didn't want to start any renovation until approval was obtained to alter the windows to allow more light in', says Gesualdi, who was held up by the local council's planning process for a number of years. 'There was no point in starting if the place was going to remain dark and oppressive', he says.

As Gesualdi wasn't permitted to alter the building's façade or change the low brick front fence, he planted a row of cypress trees to create privacy. When permission finally came through to alter the windows, the renovation proceeded slowly. Almost everything was customised by specialist artisans and tradespeople with whom Gesualdi has worked for many years.

The front forecourt, enclosed in black steel, creates another layer to the building. A steel canopy, punctuated by three circular skylights, provides a 'breathing space' before entering the building. Complete with a 4-metre-tall pivotal door, the steel forecourt is moody, emphasising the original features of the building, including oversized Art Deco wall lights that frame the entrance and stylised timber and chrome front doors. The installation of the steel canopy drew the focus away from the relatively plain brick façade.

MOODY ENTRANCE

According to Gesualdi, the Art Deco period is synonymous with symmetry – but this was not evident in the building prior to the renovation. Doors to the rooms on either side of the passage were not aligned and were made of solid timber, making the entrance oppressive. As well as repositioning the openings, Gesualdi replaced them with steel-and-bevelled-glass doors. He painted the walls a black-brown hue, a colour commonly used on bridges, often as an undercoat. Delicate wall lights designed by Fortuni add to the atmosphere and create a decorative touch, something that wouldn't have appeared in the original utilitarian scheme.

The pièce de résistance of the home/office is a three-level steel staircase, sculptured to perfection like Michelangelo's *David* in the photomontage positioned directly behind it. Designed by Gesualdi and fabricated by Peter Drofenik, the combination of the two

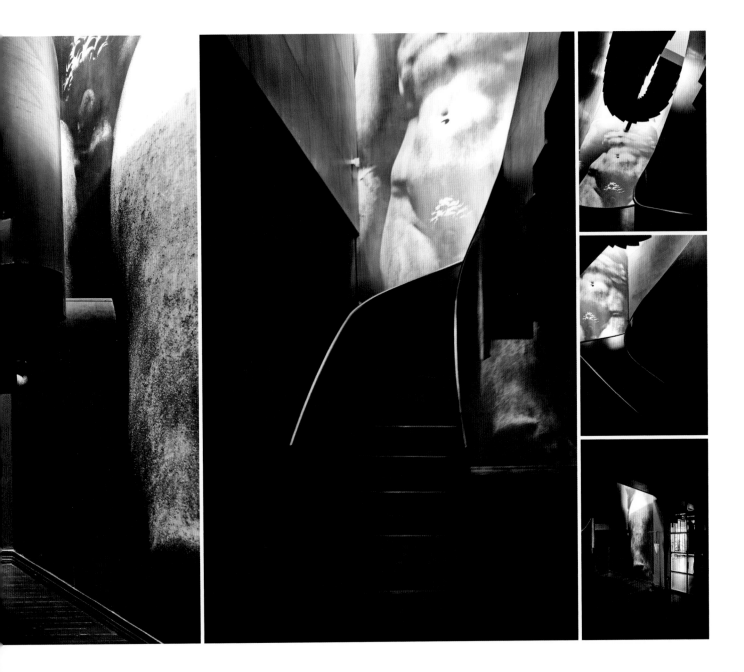

creates a powerful statement. 'For me, everything starts in Florence (where the original David sculpture stands). I lived there and also worked there for several years', says Gesualdi, who owned a chain of fashion boutiques in the 1970s through to the '90s. 'Fashion has been an important part of my life. Everything I do – whether its architecture, furniture, or homeware – relates to human proportions', says Gesualdi, who regularly has a tape measure in hand.

THE SALON

On one side of the passage, Gesualdi has retained all the features of what was previously the mess hall. Lined with leadlight cabinets of Queensland oak and built-in seats/ storage units, the space is now referred to as 'the salon'. Some of the timber had been painted. Other timber had several layers of varnish, making the grain almost invisible. Even the decorative stone fireplace had been painted. Gesualdi stripped the fireplace

with acid to remove paint and scorch marks. To lighten the palette he installed a large, unadorned, mirrored over-mantle.

In contrast, the dry bar leading from the salon was relatively easy to rework. One of the main changes to this area was the addition of glass-panelled doors leading to the garden. With the view to a manicured lawn and mature hedge restored, the vision is reminiscent of a scene from Peter Greenaway's film, *The Draftsman's Contract*. 'You can see why I didn't start the renovation until the council approval came through to change the glass in the windows and create new doors', emphasises Gesualdi. In homage to the room's history as a place to drink, Gesualdi designed a steel cabinet/bar suspended from the wall.

On the other side of the entrance are offices and a showroom. These areas have been touched only lightly, with the cement walls painted white and skirting boards left intact. The original frosted glass and timber doors were also retained, as well as the

built-in joinery. One of the storerooms was converted into a kitchen for staff. Featuring stainless steel benches and splashbacks, this area includes a laundry concealed behind painted MDF doors. The space is quite simple, with the raw concrete floors slightly cracked through years of wear.

TROMPE L'OEIL

One of the main challenges of the renovation was creating a sense of containment in what is actually only a portion of a considerably larger building. While the sculptural steel staircase creates vertical space, there was originally a solid brick wall at the back of the lobby. Gesualdi removed the wall and replaced the bricks with faux steel and bevelled-glass doors on either side of the staircase. He also retained built-in seating and stylised wall motifs framing the lobby. This device creates the sense of a space beyond this point. In effect, the doors create a trompe l'oeil effect.

Also on ground level is a guest bedroom, originally lined with rows of showers and basins for soldiers. Completely reworked, this bedroom now includes honed basalt floors (replacing a terrazzo floor) and walls, together with an open ensuite and dressing area. Even the freestanding basin in the ensuite is clad in basalt, as though chiselled from the floor. The basalt tiles were customised to the square metre to achieve the desired effect.

While Michelangelo's *David* towers over the staircase, the image has been dulled to ensure his muscular physique isn't overwhelming. Nevertheless, the space at the top of the stairs leaves people breathless. The vast open-plan space – comprising kitchen, dining and living areas – is framed by glazed windows and doors. Before the renovation, there was only one door to the terrace. However, one reason for creating new openings was to make the most of the city views and northern aspect. 'The original layout felt like a little suburban apartment with most of the rooms enclosed. There was even an enclosed verandah at the front', adds Gesualdi.

CUSTOMISED TO THE NTH DEGREE

The entire first floor of the building was gutted and, rather than creating new walls, Gesualdi used the U-shaped floor plan to define the spaces. On one side of the stairwell is the kitchen. Designed by Gesualdi and manufactured in Italy, the kitchen joinery took several months to arrive. With joinery and benches made entirely from stainless steel, the drawers open to reveal timber-lined shelves with an extensive range of implements. All the knives and utensils came with the unit and each has its own nook in its own drawer. And to ensure each plate size can be accommodated, drawers are fitted with timber pegs (capable of being reconfigured) to ensure plates remain fixed rather than moving around.

One of the few kitchen items not made in Italy was the stainless steel range hood suspended over the island bench. Designed to disappear into the ceiling cavity with

the touch of a switch, it was conceived to ensure sight lines were not diminished while cooking. Similarly, a retractable power point column is integral to the island bench to reduce untidy cords. The kitchen elements were designed more as pieces of furniture than traditional joinery. To create a streamlined effect, the refrigerator and pantry are concealed behind stainless steel doors.

A TOUCH OF FLORENCE

One of the most coveted areas of the terrace is a tent-like structure on its northern edge. Lined with citrus trees, the terrace offers the sense that one could easily be in Florence. 'It's a wonderful space, either during the day or at night when the city backdrop really comes alive', says Gesualdi.

The dining area, adjacent to the kitchen, features a striking, oval, black steel table with oversized Baroque-style timber legs. Designed by Gesualdi, it is as considered as the freeform modular foam lounge in the living area. Polished plaster walls, termed 'stucco lustro', are void of art, allowing the spaces to be the focal point. 'I'm not interested in clutter. I'd prefer to have a few key pieces of furniture', he adds.

A CONCEALED DOOR

Creating an element of surprise is important for Gesualdi, who prefers that not everything be discovered at once. A second bedroom leading from the living area could almost be missed. Featuring a door clad in basalt, it reads as part of the living room walls.

The attic-style main bedroom on the top level of the building is yet another surprise, with David's head appearing at the top of the stairs. Previously, this area was unused space. However, Gesualdi stood on a ladder and saw the views he'd been missing out on by keeping it vacant. So to connect the attic with the living areas below, he created

a double-height void above the dining area. Black glass balustrades framing the attic bedroom link the two levels, as well as reflecting additional light.

The pitched glass roof in this attic bedroom allows views of the sky and features operable windows to purge hot air during the warmer months. As with the other two bedrooms, the ensuite bathroom is an extension of the space.

THE HUMAN SCALE

Gesualdi, who trained as an architect, has a clear vision of what he wants to achieve in design. After decades of designing for others, both in fashion and architecture, his senses are honed. 'My years in fashion have helped me enormously. Whether I'm designing a chair or an interior, it's about understanding the human scale. Understanding the way something is draped on the body requires the same skill as understanding the way someone sits in a chair or enters a room. You know when something is just right', he adds.

AN ORGANIC APPROACH

Circa 1936

Original architect: Leslie Wilkinson
Remodel: Luigi Rosselli (architect)
and Interni (interior design)

EUROPEAN INFLUENCE

Originally designed by Leslie Wilkinson in 1936, this house appears to ramble up its steep slope. Located in Double Bay, Sydney, it has a strong European feel. Not surprisingly, Wilkinson, the first professor of architecture at the University of Sydney, travelled extensively throughout Europe in the early 20th century before coming to Australia. French doors, generous terraces, pergolas and balconies all feature in this Mediterranean-style house.

FLATS IMPINGING ON THE VIEWS

Originally the Wilkinson house enjoyed unimpeded views of the harbour. Unfortunately, a block of flats was built next door four years after the house was completed. These flats not only significantly impeded on the view, but also the northern light. When the current owner, Francis, bought the house in the early 1980s, it wasn't the full Wilkinson vision.

However, with his wife Lisa, he has slowly transformed the house into a magical family home for them and their three children.

Reworked by architect Luigi Rosselli and interior designer Louise Bell, director of Interni, the house was only marginally extended at the rear of the site. 'Wilkinson built the house like a Rubik's cube. All the different levels interlock. But from the outset, Wilkinson's design developed organically', says Rosselli.

SEAHORSE MOTIF

While the house originally featured a stepped garden to maximise the water views, it is now densely planted to partially camouflage the neighbouring flats. Landscape designer Andrew Pfeiffer included a number of exotic as well as local species in the garden, while retaining the tiered sandstone walls. Enthusiasts of Wilkinson's work visiting the house might be impressed that the front gate has also been retained. However, the gate set within a stone archway is actually a replica based on Wilkinson's original design,

complete with seahorse motif. This motif was often used by Wilkinson, who had a penchant for whimsical details.

ON ARRIVAL

Although the house sits on a relatively steep incline, the steps leading to the front door are generous and widely spaced. Rather than being overwhelming, the front door is framed by a modest portico. A timber door with glass panes arranged in a herringbone pattern greets visitors. Originally, this was a solid timber door. But with the encroachment of the flats, the owners were keen to lighten the interior.

POLISHED CONCRETE FLOORS

The first sign of Wilkinson's visionary approach can be seen in the entrance to the home. Polished concrete floors lead to a staircase, also with concrete treads. Instead of heavy skirting boards lining the staircase, a fine continuous groove has been etched into the

polished plaster walls. With these details pared back, the emphasis is on the wrought iron staircase, with its curvaceous handrail and medallion-shaped motifs. 'With most staircases, you're aware of the effort in changing level. But this house is designed around half-levels', says Rosselli.

NEW LIFE FOR A GARAGE

One of the architect's seamless changes occurs on the landing of the first half-level, where the formal living area is located. On the other side, the staircase leads to the original garage, which is now used as a children's music/rumpus room. While the staircase leading to the music room appears original, it's one of the subtle changes made to the house. Previously the music room was accessible only from the outside. A powder room on the stairwell landing was removed and new concrete stairs were added. 'I really didn't appreciate sitting in the lounge and looking directly into a powder room.

The children also needed a place they could make as much noise as they liked', says Lisa. Rather than disguise what was once the garage, the original features, including the concrete ceiling and distinctive pattern in the garage door, have been retained. However, new built-in bookshelves were added, along with a couple of additional side windows to increase the amount of light. To compensate for the loss of a garage (which wasn't large enough for two cars), Rosselli created a new two-car garage, as well as a generous wine cellar.

REMOVING DOORS

To increase the amount of light in the home, as well as creating more fluid spaces, Rosselli removed the solid timber doors in the entrance leading to the kitchen and living areas. He also increased the openings to ceiling height. For added reflection, the walls in the entrance and framing the stairwell were applied with stucco lustro (polished plaster).

According to the owners, the house was originally designed for a doctor and his wife, whose sister was the renowned interior designer Marion Hall Best, who pigmented the home's plastered walls. Unfortunately, Hall Best's efforts had been covered up with paint and couldn't be saved.

FORMAL LIVING ROOM

Luckily, many features in the Double Bay house could be restored. The square-shaped fireplace in the oval-shaped formal living area simply needed to be rejuvenated with a new coat of paint. All of the French-style windows and doors leading to the terrace were also in relatively good condition. Unfortunately, the timber shutters framing most of the windows had rotted over time. These were replaced with new shutters, in the same style as Wilkinson's.

Originally the ceiling in the formal living area was made from Canite, a fibre made from pressed sugar cane. When one central light fitting required replacement, it entailed

replacing the entire ceiling. A hole left by the central pendant couldn't be patched. 'Some things appeared quite easy to replace. But others, like the ceiling, became far more complicated than initially thought', says Rosselli. One of the simpler tasks was creating a new steel balustrade on the living room terrace to meet building regulations. Rosselli took his cue from Wilkinson, including in the detail a seahorse motif. Also in line with Wilkinson's design, tiles on the terrace were removed to reveal the original concrete surface. Other details in the living room were conceived to bring additional light to the stairwell. Bell, for example, created a lattice-style window adjacent to the fireplace.

ENSUITES WELL BEFORE THEIR TIME

Another half-level above the formal lounge is the main bedroom with ensuite and a terrace. Almost intact, this bedroom still contains the original built-in joinery across one entire wall. Wilkinson was also ahead of his time when it came to ensuite bathrooms. Separated by a few timber stairs, the ensuite bathroom was completely reworked for contemporary living.

CHILDREN'S LEVEL

Another half-flight of stairs leads to the children's wing. Comprising three bedrooms and two bathrooms, this area features a new skylight. Originally the owners wanted a hatch-style structure over the top landing to bring additional light into the home, as well as purge hot air during the warmer months. However, the local council claimed the structure would be detected from the street. While the hatch wasn't realised, operable windows above doorways to the children's bedrooms were, allowing a continual stream of air. Like the other levels, the children's rooms also lead to balconies.

REWORKING THE LIVING SPACES

One of the main changes to Wilkinson's design was the configuration of the kitchen and living areas. The kitchen, in the day of servants, was tucked away and accessed via a side entrance. And the formal dining room, although not large by today's standards, was surrounded by doorways. To remedy this, the scullery was converted into a laundry

and one of the doorways was filled in to create a more intimate space. The additional wall space also allowed more room for the owners to display their art collection. 'We wanted to create the spirit of Wilkinson's design without trying to mimic his work', says Rosselli. Rather than completing the renovation in one fell swoop, it was carefully staged over a number of years. Initially there was a brief for a pool and pool house, together with a detached library; then a family room was added. Following this renovation, the stairwell was connected to the original garage, now a rumpus room. Finally, a new garage was designed. These stages are in keeping with Wilkinson's organic approach to design, with rooms appearing to grow naturally according to a client's needs.

The kitchen and informal living areas also needed upgrading. Bell designed an undulating joinery unit adjacent to the kitchen, which allows crockery and utensils to be displayed. What was a porch leading to a scullery is now a laundry as well as a walk-in pantry. Although the new kitchen is contemporary, with a Cararra marble island bench and splashbacks, it doesn't overwhelm Wilkinson's design in terms of material or scale.

Tallow wood floors feature in all of these living spaces and where new windows or doors were required, their scale was rendered sympathetic to the original.

A CLEAR DIVISION BETWEEN PAST AND PRESENT

One of the clearest divisions between past and present is the family room adjacent to the kitchen. Two new glass doors frame this space, and there's a glass skylight separating the kitchen from the family room. The owners wanted a view of their garden, but they were also keen to access the terrace from a number of directions. 'It was quite difficult finding sufficient space for the family room. We had to remove quite a lot of rock from the base of the cliff face', says Rosselli.

LIBRARY

As well as the family room, the detached office/library is entirely new. Constructed from sandstone, like the retaining walls in the garden, the library follows the curves

in Wilkinson's design. Lined with floor-to-ceiling shelves and framed by French doors, the library allows the adults solitude and a level of separation from children's activities. However, rather than feeling disconnected from the surrounds, sandstone floor tiles used in the library extend to the terrace, with its original concrete pillars and new timber pergola designed in the manner of Wilkinson.

POOL HOUSE

As the property is on a substantial incline, Rosselli was keen to maximise the outdoor areas. Above the library is a terrace, currently being developed as a vegetable garden. Another set of stairs leads to a lap pool and detached pool house. Enclosed by glass doors that can be pulled right back to allow for an open verandah, the pool house, like the rest of the house, features iconic chairs, predominantly from the 20th century. While Rosselli and his clients had few differences, the pillars lining the pool house did create some lengthy discussion. Lisa wanted to be able to see the children swimming

while sitting in the pool house. However, while a view through the pillars was possible, it made overseeing the children a little more difficult. 'Luigi wanted them an equal distance apart, like most architects. But as you can see, they're more random', says Lisa.

A SMALL STUMBLING BLOCK

Getting approval for the pool house from the local council had its own problems. A vineyard established more than 150 years ago was once part of the property. While there were no longer any signs of vines, there was a rudimentary map from the 1830s. 'It was roughly drawn. Even so, at one stage, we didn't think we'd get our pool house or our pool', says Lisa, who continually marvels at both Wilkinson and Rosselli's work. 'Every time I walk up and down the stairs, I feel like I'm in a seashell', adds Lisa, caressing the lustrous curved walls.

1940-19

49

The 1940s represented a fascinating time for architecture. With materials in short supply after the Second World War, architects came up with ingenious solutions rather than simply producing lavish homes. In many ways, there was a renaissance in Australian architecture, particularly in the later part of this decade, with open-plan designs capturing the essence of the native bush settings. Many of the homes built during this period were influenced by the efforts of engineers such as Bill Irwin, who made many homes appear to float.

SOMETHING WITH CHARACTER

Circa 1940   Original architect: Geoffrey Sommers
Remodel: Inarc Architects

RETURNING FROM LONDON

The owners of this house in Toorak, Melbourne, had been living in London for almost ten years. However, with family in Victoria and two young children, they decided to return. 'We were looking for something with character, but a house that we could add our own stamp to', says Cate, who lives in this house with her husband David and their children, Arabella and Otto.

While in London, the couple had renovated a couple of apartments. These homes were originally built in the Victorian period, but renovated in a contemporary and minimal style by London-based architect Voon Wong. As mentioned by David, they were interested in achieving a clean and contemporary look.

BACK TO AUSTRALIA

Although David and Cate had more than sufficient space in their London apartment, they were looking for a larger and detached home with a garden on their return to

Australia. Although they weren't exactly sure what type of house they were looking for, they didn't want a Victorian or Edwardian period home. 'We find many of these homes too fussy in their detail. We generally prefer a more pared-back aesthetic', says David. 'Those homes can often be quite dark', he adds.

GRAND FINAL

David and Cate initially found their Toorak house on the Web, shortly after they arrived back in Melbourne. Fortunately, the house was being auctioned on Grand Final day for the Australian Football League, something that virtually brings the nation to a halt. No other bidders seriously interested in the property turned up, with not one bid given on the day (a tip for those wishing to buy a house without any rival bidders).

The lack of interest may well have been a result of the football. It could also have been due the condition of the house, particularly the decorative touches from the 1980s. Powder-blue carpets dotted the house and the kitchen bench tops were granite.

The pièce de résistance was the peach-coloured spa bath in the main bathroom, while the rear extension, built in the 1960s, didn't improve the situation.

APPROPRIATE SCALE

Although the house fronts one of the suburb's grandest boulevards, this house, originally designed by Geoffrey Sommers, is relatively modest in scale compared with some of the neighbouring mansions. 'I was quite surprised at the size of the rooms and the intimacy of their scale when I first came to inspect the house', says interior designer Christopher Hansson, who worked closely with architect Reno Rizzo, both directors of Inarc Architects. 'We could see there was great potential', he adds.

One of the spaces that had been ignored by the previous owners was the attic. The roof's substantial pitched cavity contained six large copper water tanks. David and Cate compared the size of this attic to the size of a typical London flat and approaching the area of many homes in Tokyo.

CLEAN AND MINIMAL LINES

Although London and Tokyo have generally smaller abodes than Australia, particularly in the inner city, Cate and David appreciate clean and minimal architectural lines wherever they happen to be. They had seen this quality in Inarc's work, in magazines and on their website. They also inspected one of Inarc's houses. 'Their work reminded us of Wong's', says Cate.

BORROWING VIEWS

Rizzo could see beyond the powder-blue carpet and other 1980s embellishments. As well as having 'great bones', the house benefited from verdant outlooks (a new garden was created by designer Jack Merlo). The neighbouring house's terracotta shingles create one impressive vista from the living areas. 'It's about borrowing views from neighbours' gardens', says Rizzo, pointing out the lush forest in an adjoining property.

Inarc Architects are known for their new contemporary homes, but they are equally interested in renovating existing homes, provided there is a certain chemistry between client and architect. And while many architects prefer to clearly delineate the past from the present, Inarc sees the challenge as marrying the two periods together. 'In many ways it's more challenging combining the two together', says Hansson.

A MARRIAGE OF STYLES

This 'marriage' of two styles can be seen in Inarc's treatment of the windows. In the study/guest bedroom at the front of the house, each window comprises six window panes. In contrast, but sympathetic to the original windows, the glass-and-steel windows and doors in the new wing also feature glass panes. But the new panes are considerably larger and the steel detailing is evocative of the 1940s.

Some of the challenges facing Inarc Architects not only included achieving their clients' spatial requirements, but also replacing most of the basic services, including new plumbing,

electrical work, as well as structural changes. 'People underestimate the cost of replacing these services. It's usually a considerable amount of money and it's something that people don't stand back and admire', says Rizzo.

KITCHEN AND LIVING AREAS

One of the largest expenses was creating a new kitchen and informal living area at the rear of the house. While the two areas are combined, the designers delineated the two spaces by increasing the ceiling height in the informal living area to just under 4 metres. To bring in the outdoors from all aspects, as well as increasing the light, Inarc included highlight celestial windows. Verdant outdoor views are now obtained from all aspects, and a new lawn garden replaces a swimming pool. Water tanks are concealed below the lawn.

Stained American oak flooring extends throughout the kitchen and living areas, with recessed hydronic heating (as well as cooling) in the floor being both thermally effective and eliminating bulky units. Other thoughtful features in the kitchen/living area include a built-in desk, positioned in a bay-like nook. Similarly considered is the laundry/butler's pantry, protruding into the home's side pathway to maximise space.

A MINIMAL TOUCH

While the kitchen, with its extensive built-in joinery, forms part of the home's new wing, the dining area is located under the original roofline. Like the adjoining formal lounge, one of the main tasks for Rizzo and Hansson was removing some of the superfluous detail. The fireplace in the lounge, for example, has a John Pawson-like minimal touch. While there are new skirting boards in the formal areas, these are square-edged,

creating a contemporary outline. Unlike many homes of this period, window furnishings have been completely eliminated, sharpening the focus on the garden. The neutral painted walls also provide a canvas for the couple's collection of Indigenous Australian art, including the work of William King Jungala. 'We found many of our paintings and sculpture through Jennifer Dudley of Outback Aboriginal Art', says Cate.

RESPECTING THE PAST

To create a more relaxed feel to the formal living areas, Inarc designed a wall of built-in bookshelves. This allows the dining area to be used as a reading area during the day, rather than simply when guests come for dinner. Unlike many period homes, which can be quite regimented in their arrangement, this house includes some of its own quirks. Sets of paned windows don't follow a strict pattern and doorways aren't always aligned with adjoining rooms. One of the main discussions held with the owners was whether or not to retain the original turned timber balustrades of the staircase. Fortunately,

these were retained; however, when a new staircase was required to connect the first floor with the attic, Inarc came up with a contemporary design – the turned timber rails replaced with simple clean lines of white timber posts. From the doorway, the subtle change in style, as well as the additional staircase, creates an effect similar to an M.C. Escher image.

BEDROOMS

On the first floor of the house are the bedrooms, including the main bedroom with a walk-in dressing area and ensuite bathroom. On this level are also the two children's bedrooms, together with a bathroom. One of the discoveries made during the renovation was the original doorway to the ensuite bathroom in the main bedroom. As plaster was removed, it became apparent that the location of the doorway had changed, post-1940. Repositioning the door not only created greater privacy in the bathroom, but also allowed for increased light.

As well as letting in abundant light, the absence of window dressing allows for views of the moss-covered terracotta shingles of a neighbouring home. These beautiful shingles, with all their moss and lichen, were a drawcard for the couple when they first saw the house. So when it came to creating a new carport, they went to recycling yards and found almost identical shingles, fortunately also covered with moss.

THE ATTIC

One of the most valuable areas of the house in terms of usage is the attic. It was first discovered by David when he climbed a ladder and poked his head through a hatch. 'I just thought the space was extraordinary, not only in terms of size, but also the volume', says David, referring to its pitched silhouette. The old copper boilers were removed by Inarc Architects and the attic converted into a guest wing, with a study

separating a bedroom at one end and a living area at the other. Although David has a study on the ground floor, he sometimes works in the attic when complete quiet is required.

This house is extremely comfortable and spacious. However, unlike many McMansions built today, the scale of each room is intimate, rather than overwhelming. Although the house is of its period, it offers the same clean and minimal lines found in the finest contemporary architecture. 'These spaces aren't designed to impress. They're here to enjoy', says David.

SOMETHING WITH CHARACTER

DOUGLAS SNELLING HOUSE

Circa 1948

Original architect: Douglas Snelling
Remodel: Tzannes Associates

This award-winning house in Northbridge, Sydney (recipient of the Wilkinson Award and the Robyn Boyd Award) isn't detectable from the street. However, locals as well as architecture enthusiasts are well aware of its existence. Designed in 1948 by renowned architect Douglas Snelling, the cliff-side home descends over several levels to Middle Harbour.

When the current owners John and Di bought this house in 1991, Douglas Snelling wasn't at the forefront of their minds. However, the couple was extremely familiar with the postwar period of design in Australia, with John's parents having commissioned the eminent architect Neville Gruzman to design a family home for them in Bellevue Hill. 'How could you forget that period', says Di, recalling Gruzman's seamless treatment of indoor and outdoor spaces, together with the bravado shown by many designers from that time. 'It felt like coming home', she adds.

A HOUSE THAT SUITED

In 1991, John, Di and their two adult daughters weren't living in one of these postwar architectural gems. The family was living in a cottage in Killara, and while they had added a second storey, it was never completely finished (maybe a sign that it wasn't quite the house they were after). 'Our youngest daughter kept saying that nothing in the house worked properly and that any furniture never really suited, that she was going to look out for a new house', says Di.

The previous owner of the Snelling house, celebrated cellist Nathan Wax, had rented it out while he was overseas. A small advertisement in a local newspaper caught Di's daughter's eye. The Northbridge house was in relatively poor condition, with a few unsympathetic additions such as a thatched roof cabana by the pool. However, it was evident that the design was significant and a jewel waiting to be polished. As was discovered, the house was originally designed as Snelling's own family home, but unfortunately his family never moved in.

When John, Di and their two daughters moved into the house, there was a little self-doubt. Some family and friends raised eyebrows. Di's father thought the house was rather monastic, with its internal stone walls. Others thought the concrete stairs leading to the house would eventually cause the family concern. 'From the start, we didn't see ourselves as purists, wanting to completely restore the house. We couldn't have lived with the bathrooms the way they were. Some of the plumbing was completely shot', says Di.

The couple spoke to a number of architects about reworking parts of the house. While some architects were keen to put their own strong imprint on Snelling's design, others, such as Alex Tzannes, director of Tzannes Associates, recognised the significance of the house. 'John and Di didn't really know much about Snelling before they bought the house', says Tzannes, 'but they realised the house needed considerable work. There were a few shortcomings as materials were in short supply after the war. It was

all there. It just needed restoring and rehabilitating. There was never any intention of doing a completely new scheme. Some areas just hadn't been fully detailed', says Tzannes.

As well as bracing the building and making sure the house was structurally sound, a number of the roof structures had to be completely redesigned to eliminate flooding. 'Some of Snelling's details were quite chunky. You can see the difference', says Tzannes, pointing out the differences in some of the column sizes between past and present.

ON STAGE

Access to the house is via a sweeping concrete driveway leading to a carport. Framed by sandstone walls and an angular 'floating' roof, it's the first sign of the architectural gem waiting to be discovered. A set of concrete stairs leads to the front door, past what appears to be a self-contained guest suite. In fact, the sandstone building formed part of Snelling's original scheme. Complete with a stage, this building was used by Northbridge's Musical Society during the 1950s. Tzannes restored the stage and it

is now used as a home theatre. The owners' daughter, a film producer, also uses this space when she's working in Sydney (she is normally based in New York).

A SENSE OF ARRIVAL

As in many of his architectural works, in this house Snelling created a sense of suspense upon entering. As well as the sculptural staircase, with its fluid timber handrail, Snelling included a pond and fern garden at the entrance to the house. Originally there were two entrances: one leading to the main house, the other to the parents' retreat, including the main bedroom. However, when Di and John arrived, their preference was for one entrance.

Over a bridge, the front door opens to reveal a modest lobby. At this level are the main bedroom, ensuite and walk-in dressing area connected to a large terrace by large sliding glass doors. Originally this area consisted of two bedrooms, but they have been opened to create one generous space offering idyllic views of the harbour. Although the bathrooms associated with the two former bedrooms existed in Snelling's design, they have been

reworked by Tzannes. Only some of these spaces required modification, which included adding a highlight window in the dressing area for additional light, as well as to provide a glimpse of the majestic gum trees on the water's edge. One of Tzannes' additions was creating a canopy over the terrace. Skillion-shaped and evocative of the period, this awning allows for protection from the weather while still allowing sunlight to penetrate.

'I wanted the original and new work to be easily distinguishable from each other. You should be able to clearly "read" the different layers', says Tzannes.

RECONFIGURING SPACES

On the other side of the top level is what was previously designated as Snelling's retreat. Featuring two bedrooms – one with a sandstone fireplace that forms a continuous band to the fireplace in the formal lounge – both spaces are light-filled. One of these bedrooms

includes a built-in wardrobe and dressing table. Snelling was also a leader when it came to designer furniture – his contoured 'Web' chair is considered an iconic piece.

Given the level of experimentation in this house, it's not surprising that Tzannes had a challenge ahead. In one of the bedrooms on the top level is a butterfly-shaped roof, poised as if about to take flight. While this ingenious design provided additional light, it also caused significant water problems.

LIVING AREAS

On the middle level of the house, accessed via timber stairs and timber feature wall, are the main living areas. This space includes the formal lounge and dining area, separated by a massive sandstone fireplace. Both the lounge and dining areas feature exposed, chunky timber beams. There's also a kitchen with 'back of house' amenities, such as a laundry, a bathroom and also a workroom. One of the main changes to this

level was the kitchen. Tzannes refrained from creating a standout contemporary kitchen. He loosely retained the original configuration in the kitchen, but extended the area to include sufficient area for a pantry. While the timber cupboards, as well as the stainless steel bench tops and rubber floors are new, these materials capture perfectly the essence of Snelling's original design. The original frosted glass highlight windows were also retained, together with the windows and fixtures. Subtle additions include a bullnose-shaped lip on the edge of the bench separating the dining area, evocative of Snelling's approach. Other appropriate responses include open-steel-mesh drawers.

REFLECTIVE POND

The house is literally surrounded by nature, including a wonderful vista of ferns from John's study (originally designed as a rumpus room), and Snelling seemed keen to bring a sense of the outdoors inside the home. Adjacent to the formal living area is

a reflective pond, framed by a series of glass panels designed by artist Janet Lawrence. Originally this enclosed space was a courtyard, planted with ferns. 'The ferns were always straining to reach the light. Alec thought the area would be better suited for water', says Di. 'Janet's glass reflects the landscape', she adds.

Like the reflective pond, the formal living area has a meditative quality. With large sliding glass doors to the terrace, and views over the water, there's a sense of tranquillity. 'You almost feel as though you're sitting in a cave, but it's not that feeling of being enclosed', says Di. Changes were made to the terrace leading from the lounge. Originally finished in crazy-paved sandstone and spread over two levels, it was widened to create one level and finished in sandstone tiles. Previously the two levels caused an awkward arrangement of outdoor furniture, with Di and John concerned that dinner guests may tip their chairs over the edge.

GUEST WING

One of the most substantial changes made to the Northbridge house was the addition of an entirely new level below the living areas. Tzannes Associates excavated to create this level, conceived as an independent guest wing. Like the main kitchen, this kitchen features American ash cupboards and stainless steel benchtops, and as with the other two levels, it has its own terrace. In keeping with the period, there are Arne Jacobsen dining chairs and a vivid lounge suite by Pierre Paulin.

While the house is a large home for a couple (their children stay only intermittently), Di and John aren't overwhelmed by the spaces. 'We use the entire living areas every day. And in winter, the sun literally comes to the edge of the living areas. In summer, it's extremely cool' says Di. 'It's just such a beautiful home. We have both Douglas and Alex to thank for that', she adds.

DOUGLAS SNELLING HOUSE

DOUGLAS SNELLING HOUSE

DOUGLAS SNELLING HOUSE

INDEX OF ARCHITECTS AND INTERIOR DESIGNERS